Are you ready to discover
how 10 minutes
a day could
change your life?

The 28 Day Meditation Challenge has given me the ability to have some time of complete peacefulness, allowing me to centre myself and become calmer.

Thank you for helping me along the way.

Charlotte

The 28 Day Meditation Challenge helped me re-focus and find a peaceful moment in the day. It felt like I had a reassuring hand on my shoulder, willing me to find ten minutes a day to find peace.

The change in my mental attitude is remarkable.

Alex

The 28 Day Meditation Challenge was just what I needed to get myself refocused and calm before quite a hectic time.

Thank you Clare.

Joy

I did the 28 Day Meditation Challenge and it made me feel like I had a kind and firm hand on my shoulders.

I felt reassured that all was well. I felt a deep peacefulness and 'in the moment'.

Sharon

I did the 28 Day Meditation Challenge and realised that, even after doing intensive 10-day retreats, ten minutes a day is enough to have a massive impact!

Star

The 28 Day Meditation Challenge was a deeply personal, much-needed exercise that I looked forward to on a daily basis.

Although done in the comfort of my own home (and alone), I felt a sense of inclusion, reading the daily messages, and a sense of involvement in something powerful and far-reaching.

Nick

After reading today's message from the 28 Day Meditation Challenge, I chatted with my husband. He understands how important it is for me to have ME time, to meditate. Thank you for inspiring me to ask for his help with this. It's been very useful.

Busy mum of young children

If this is how I feel after my very first attempt, I can't wait to see how I am at the end of the 28 Day Meditation Challenge!

Phil

I wasn't a believer in this kind of thing, but having done the 28 Day Meditation Challenge I have changed my mind completely.

C.L.

Clare Josa really walks the talk. She is a centre of calm in a raging world.

I could not recommend her more highly to lead you on your journey of meditation, mindfulness and deep relaxation.

Dr Steve Williams

First published by Beyond Alchemy Publishing in 2012

This 2nd edition: April 2013

www.BeyondAlchemyPublishing.co.uk

© Clare Josa 2012

ISBN 978-1-908854-31-5

A catalogue record for this book is available from the British Library.

The right of Clare Josa to be identified as the author of this work has been asserted in accordance with the Copyright, Designs and Patents Act of 1988.

All rights reserved.

No part of this publication may be reproduced, stored in a retrieval system, or transmitted in any form or by any means, electronic, mechanical, photocopying, recording or otherwise, without the prior permission of the author.

Cover design by Paul Michael Wilson www.designbypmw.com

The advice in this book is intended for educational purposes only and it is not intended to substitute for professional medical advice. In the event that you use any of this information for yourself, the publisher and author accept no responsibility for your actions. Always consult your medical professional, if you are unsure about whether any of the suggested techniques are suitable for you.

28 Day Meditation Challenge

Discover how 10 minutes a day can change your life.

Clare Josa

Meditation Teacher & NLP Trainer

Foreword by Dr Steve Williams

Foreword by Dr. Steve Williams 8
Acknowledgements & Gratitude 10
Where To Download The Meditations 13
How To Get The Most Out Of This Course 14
Getting Started 18
> What Is Meditation? 20
> What To Expect From The 28 Day Meditation Challenge 24
> What To Do If You Miss A Day? 31
> How Long Does It Take To Break – Or Make - A Habit? 33
> The Secret To Keeping Yourself Motivated 36

Week One 40
> Day 1: Busting The Number One Meditation Myth 42
> Day 2: Are You Sitting Comfortably? 49
> Day 3: What Are Your Favourite Meditation Excuses? 59
> Day 4: But I Don't Have Time To Meditate! 64
> Day 5: How To Get Moral Support For Your Meditation Time 71
> Day 6: What To Do If You Miss A Day 77
> Day 7: Keeping The Momentum Going 82

Week Two 88
> Day 8: Making Friends With Your Monkey Mind 90
> Day 9: How To Stop Others From Stealing Your Meditation Time 97
> Day 10: What Is Your Monkey Mind Trying To Tell You? 104
> Day 11: How To Stop Your 'To Do' List Getting In The Way 113
> Day 12: Insider Secrets: How To Create The Meditating Habit 118
> Day 13: Are You Too Tired To Meditate? 124
> Day 14: But I've Not Had Instant Results! 130

Week Three 135

    Day 15: What On Earth Is Mindfulness? 137

    Day 16: Is It Time To Taste Your Tea? 145

    Day 17: Want A Magic Wand For Worrying? 150

    Day 18: How Wiggling Your Butt Can Help You Meditate 157

    Day 19: Getting Over The Meditation Hump 162

    Day 20: How Dare You Interrupt My Meditation! 168

    Day 21: Meditation Stirs The Pot 173

Week Four 179

    Day 22: Discovering The Secret Of Kindness 181

    Day 23: What's The Most Dangerous Word A Newbie Meditator Can Use? 186

    Day 24: Two Little Words That Can Change Your Life 191

    Day 25: How Do I Know When I'm Meditating? 196

    Day 26: Are You Still Struggling To Find Time To Meditate? 201

    Day 27: How To Keep Yourself Motivated 205

    Day 28: Creating A Sanctuary For Your Meditation 210

And Finally… 216

    Day 29: What's Next? 217

Appendix A: The Meditations 220

    Meditation 1 221

    Meditation 2 224

    Meditation 3 227

    Meditation 4 230

Appendix B: Bonus Articles 233

How To Contact The Author 239

    About Clare Josa 239

Foreword by Dr. Steve Williams

Over my 25 years of practising in the healthcare field I have seen massive benefits from the practice of meditation and mindfulness on both the physical and mental wellbeing of people.

It seems to me that this would be an appropriate subject to be taught in schools as many of the chronic diseases and other ills of society, such as drug abuse and domestic violence, stem from the stresses, strains and expectations of the frenetic world that we live in.

An ability to induce calm in oneself is a fantastic discipline to practise and I would encourage everyone to at least try it.

Meditation, mindfulness and deep relaxation and the states they are capable of inducing have been shown to help many of the chronic conditions that plague modern society.

A systematic review of trials using meditation for anxiety disorders published in 2012[1] found that meditation decreased symptoms of anxiety.

Other recent studies that have shown favourable results from meditation and mindfulness as an intervention looked at:

- irritable bowel syndrome[2]
- substance abuse disorders[3]
- anxiety associated with breast cancer[4]
- tinnitus[5]
- chronic pelvic pain[6]
- depression (including Mindfulness-Based Stress Reduction)

Of course, you don't need to wait until you are suffering from one of these conditions, before discovering how meditation, mindfulness and deep relaxation could positively impact your life.

Clare Josa really walks the talk. She is a centre of calm in a raging world and I could not recommend her more highly to lead you on your journey of meditation, mindfulness and deep relaxation. Clare is a highly motivated and dynamic individual as well mother of three engaging boys all under ten years of age. She is a prolific writer, teacher and gifted healer and has the ability to communicate her wonderful gifts to all.

Once you experience the beauty and tranquillity of true deep relaxation, meditation and mindfulness you will not want to stop this journey and it will make profound differences to your mental, emotional and physical wellbeing. I wish you well on this path of enlightenment.

Dr Steve Williams

DC, DICS, FICS, FCC (paediatrics), FCC (cranio), FBCA

Dr Steve Williams is a widely experienced Doctor of Chiropractic based in Southampton who divides his time between a family based practice and travelling internationally to teach chiropractors and other health professionals chiropractic paediatrics and craniopathy. www.StJamesChiro.co.uk

Research References:

1 Chen KW et al Meditative therapies for reducing anxiety: A systematic review and a meta-analysis of randomised controlled trials. Depression and Anxiety 2012 Jul 29;(7) 545-62

2 Asare F et al Meditation over medication for irritable bowel syndrome? On exercise and alternative treatments for irritable bowel syndrome. Curr Gastroenterol Rep. 2012 Aug;14(4):283-9

3 Skanarvi S et al Mindfulness based interventions for addictive disorders: a review. Encephale. 2011 Oct;37(5):379-87

4 Monte DA et al Changes in Cerebral Blood Flow and Anxiety Associated with an 8-week Mindfulness Programme in Women with Breast Cancer. Stress Health. 2012 Dec;28(5):397-407

5 Kreuzer PM Mindfulness-and body-psychotherapy-based group treatment of chronic tinnitus: a randomized controlled pilot study. BMC Complement Altern Med. 2012 Nov 28;12(1):235

6 Fox SD et al Mindfulness meditation for women with chronic pelvic pain: a pilot study. J Reprod Med. 2011 Mar-Apr;56(3-4):158-62.

Acknowledgements & Gratitude

A huge thank you to everyone who has helped to turn this 28 Day Meditation Challenge from an online course into a book that can help people discover how ten minutes a day can change their lives.

To the team at Dru (www.DruWorldwide.com) – thank you for your wisdom and abhyasa, as you shared your inspiration, helping me to become a better teacher and an even better student.

Those of you who have taken part in the online version of the 28 Day Meditation Challenge course: thank you for joining in and for sharing your questions and your feedback so openly. This has helped me learn where you needed more input and clarification. It has been an essential part of creating this book. Your questions have taught me so much.

Those of you who have encouraged me: thank you! The 28 Day Meditation Challenge became a wonderfully vibrant project that seems to have a life of its own.

To Kit, for her ability to turn my recorded babblings into a typed manuscript, ready for editing. Had this process relied on my patience at a keyboard instead, this book would never have been created.

To Joy Shallcross, for her generosity of time and spirit, proof-reading this book and endeavouring to cure me of my addiction to commas. Her dedication and patience have saved you from a myriad of mediation and even medication, not to mention the occasional portion of nonsensical drivel. Any remaining errors are entirely my responsibility.

To Crista Cloutier, for her beautiful photographs and for creating the images that appear each day, throughout this book. Thank you for helping to inspire those who take part in this course.

To my family: thank you for not minding all the times when I absent-mindedly grabbed pen and paper to scribble notes for this book, in the middle of family life. Without your unwavering support and belief, this book wouldn't exist.

And finally, thank you to you, for choosing to take part in the 28 Day Meditation Challenge.

My deepest wish is that it helps you to move past old blocks, limiting beliefs and excuses, to easily and enjoyably create the habit of meditating, for ten minutes (or more!) each day.

After the 28 days, I hope you will feel inspired and confident to continue your meditation journey, in whichever way calls to you.

With love, Namaste,

Clare. ♡

To Peter

This book is dedicated to Peter,
without whose support I wouldn't be able to
indulge in my passion for teaching and writing.

Thank you for helping me to believe in my dreams,
so that I can help others to believe in theirs.

Where To Download The Meditations

The 28 Day Meditation Challenge comes with four meditations and a deep relaxation. These form the core of the course, with a new meditation for each of the four weeks.

To download your MP3 versions of the meditations, go to:

www.28DayMeditationChallenge.com/bonus

These include:
1. Track 1: Breath Awareness Meditation
2. Track 2: Thought Acceptance Meditation
3. Track 3: Mindfulness Meditation
4. Track 4: Gratitude Mantra Meditation
5. Track 5: Deep Relaxation & Guided Visualisation

I strongly encourage you to do this, as listening to the daily ten minute meditation will help you to make much faster progress with your meditation habit.

Prefer them on CD?

If you'd prefer a copy on CD, you can either order one at the above link or you can buy one via your favourite bookstore ('real world' or online).

The reference you need to give your book store is:

Title: 28 Day Meditation Challenge CD
Author: Clare Josa

How To Get The Most Out Of This Course

1. Work through the 'Getting Started' section, from page 17.
2. Then read a new message each day. Apply the bits that resonate for you.
3. Listen to your ten minute meditation, each day.
4. Optional - use each day's affirmation, if it resonates for you.
5. Optional - download & print each day's image, if it inspires you.
6. Optional – if you're too tired to meditate, do the bonus deep relaxation instead.
7. Smile and watch your life change.

The 28 Day Meditation Challenge book is based on the popular online course (www.28DayMeditationChallenge.com). It has been specially adapted for those of you who would prefer to work through the course on your own, rather than being part of the online forum and receiving daily email messages.

For it to work its magic for you, all you need to do is to read the message each day, apply the bits that inspire you and to do the ten minute meditation and mindfulness practices.

The meditations that you need for this course are included in the MP3s (and optional CD) which accompany this book.

They are also available as transcripts, in Appendix A. This enables you to do them in your own way, if you prefer that. If English isn't your first language, you can even translate them. You could do them from memory or record them yourself.

To download the MP3 versions of the meditations, here's where you can find them, free of charge, along with a lots of bonus articles and inspirational resources:

www.28DayMeditationChallenge.com/bonus

How This Course Works

This book is designed to guide you, step by step, through the first 28 days of creating a daily meditation practice.

It includes key meditation techniques that work for busy people, with busy lives.

There's no fluff. There's no floating. There's no chakra-gazing.

But it does offer you the chance to make simple changes that can transform your life – as those who have already completed the 28 Day Meditation Challenge have discovered.

It's all about practical, common sense techniques, based on proven, ancient spiritual practices, to lay the foundations for whichever direction you choose for your meditation in the future.

Being a certified NLP Trainer and an expert in psychology, Clare Josa has also included simple exercises and thought-provoking articles at key stages, to help you spot your old excuses and overcome your blocks about finding ten minutes a day for yourself.

This is what makes this course work.

Being taught how to meditate isn't enough;
Discovering how to create the daily habit is what makes the difference between a 'nice idea' and a life-changing experience.

It's important to work through this book, reading each day's section in turn, because the daily messages build on each other, to help you create strong foundations for your meditation practice.

If you miss a day, that's ok. Just pick up where you left off. If you want to repeat a day, that's fine too. If it takes you longer than 28 days to complete the challenge, that's ok. The main thing is that you do it.

The people who find that this 28 day challenge created deep-acting shifts for them are those who read each day's message and worked through the meditations and exercises in the order in which they are presented.

After The 28 Days

Once you have completed your 28 days, you can still use this book for daily inspiration. Simply close your eyes and ask yourself, *"What do I most need to know today?"* Open the book at random and read. You might be surprised which messages are there for you.

Are you ready to get started?

GETTING STARTED

LAYING THE FOUNDATIONS

What to expect, what not to expect and discovering the secret to keeping yourself motivated.

Getting Started

Message From The Author.

Welcome! I am going to be guiding you through the next 4 weeks.

Before we start, I'd like to say thank you for choosing to join in with this challenge. I really hope it brings you whatever you are looking for.

Let's get started!

It Doesn't Matter Where You're Starting From

Whether you're a newbie to meditation, or an old hand, wanting to rekindle the habit, the 28 Day Meditation Challenge is a great place to start.

We'll be covering the basics of:

- how to meditate
- how to make it comfortable
- how to overcome the common hurdles
- how to avoid the problems and mistakes that often cause people to give up.

Some of it may be familiar to you; some of it may be new. And I don't ask you to believe everything I say! I'll be sharing with you the techniques and strategies that I teach in my classes and workshop. And – as with my face-to-face students – all I ask is for you to 'try things on for size'. If it works for you, great. If not, how about tweaking it, so it does?

Getting Started

It is my deepest wish for you to experience that the next 28 days really make a difference to your life.

Many people who have made a commitment to regular meditation say that it helps them feel more calm; it helps them create a little sanctuary in their day, no matter how stressful life is. And whatever it is you want from the next 28 days (and you will be finding that out and getting quite clear on it by the end of this section) I really, really hope you achieve it.

My Number 1 Piece Of Advice

Don't make a big deal out of meditating! Don't stress about it. Just do it. That makes the whole process much easier.

I really hope you enjoy your 28 Day Meditation Challenge.

Namaste,

Clare. ♡

Clare Josa

Author, Meditation Teacher, NLP Trainer

Getting Started
What Is Meditation?

The answer sometimes depends on your culture, your religious beliefs and even the influence of the media, wherever you live.

Some people call it meditation. Others call it mindfulness. In many situations these two terms are inter-changeable, though there are some key differences, which we will be covering over the four weeks.

There is no one-lined answer to explain what meditation or mindfulness is, because it is such a personal experience.

However, in general:

> *Meditation is about finding inner stillness – about letting go of the drama and stresses of everyday life and re-connecting with the part of us that contains our deeper wisdom.*
> *It is about being fully aware in the present moment – truly living life, rather than just living a 'version of life', as narrated by our unconscious mind.*

What's The Difference Between Meditation And Mindfulness?

This course talks about meditation, because it encompasses meditation, mindfulness and many other techniques.

However, the term 'mindfulness' has become popular over recent years, partly due to the popularity of the various Buddhist traditions, as taught by HH The Dalai Lama and the Vietnamese Zen Master Thich Nhat Hanh, and partly because of the academic research surrounding Mindfulness-Based Stress Relief techniques, led by John Kabat-Zinn and his team.

Both meditation and mindfulness are ancient practices with broadly common goals, including:

Getting Started

- Self-awareness
- Inner peace
- Compassion

Mindfulness could be described as becoming fully aware of the present moment, including the stream of consciousness of your mind, without judging it or changing it. This naturally quietens the mind and can offer insights into the auto-pilot reactions we have been running in life. It helps us connect with the true nature of what we are experiencing – and to accept it. This can lead to a reduction in stress levels and a strong sense of inner peace and happiness.

Meditation involves concentration techniques, to focus on a particular exercise to quieten the mind. It can help us to connect with our deeper wisdom, so that we see those same auto-pilot reactions and make changes. It can help the mind to focus more clearly, slowing it down and preparing us for deep-acting techniques. Of course, these are simplified descriptions, but they give you an idea of the commonly-accepted meanings of the two words. Meditation and mindfulness are complementary – there is a huge overlap.

There are so many ways of practising meditation and mindfulness. There is no right or wrong way (unless your chosen belief system tells you otherwise). But there are practical ways to lay the foundations that will work more effectively for us in our over-busy Western culture – and that's what this book is about.

For the purposes of this course, I will be using the term 'meditation' to describe whichever practice we are exploring, unless it is a specific, recognised mindfulness technique. The 28 Day Meditation Challenge brings you a gentle blend of both meditation and mindfulness.

For example, mindfulness techniques are woven into the sitting meditations and meditative concentration techniques are woven into the week 3 mindfulness exercises.

Getting Started
The Benefits Of Meditation

The benefits of meditation are well documented. Even scientists are now agreeing with what meditators have known for thousands of years.

- It is common sense that **sitting quietly for ten minutes** or more each day will help us **feel more calm** and help us to **de-stress**.

- It can also **give us more clarity in life**, because we are training our mind - the Monkey Mind - the chattering mind - to **concentrate**, to **relax** and to **focus**. It can help us to **de-clutter our thoughts**, impacting everything else that we do.

- It can help us **feel happier**, because we are learning to **accept life** as it is and understanding **how we impact our experience of life**.

- We are practising exercises that help us to **let go of the things that cause us pain and the things that stress us**. Meditation has been clinically proven to have a **positive impact on the hormones** that cause the physiological and emotional experiences of stress.

- Scientists have now proven that **meditation makes your brain grow**! They have studied people who do simple mindfulness meditation exercises, even for a short period of time each day, and they have found that it physically alters your brain. It helps you to feel happier.

- Doctors are even using **mindfulness meditation to help people suffering from depression**. It is proving to be at least as effective as medication for many patients.

- Regular meditation has been proven to be **good for your heart**. Want to know more? There's a bonus article on the website: *"3 Secrets Your Heart Wants You To Know About Meditation"*. www.28DayMeditationChallenge.com/bonus

Regular meditation helps you feel less stressed; it helps you enjoy life more and, whatever your reasons for meditating, regular practice is likely to bring you the benefits that you are hoping for.

One of the side effects of regular meditation, though, is that it often allows you to become who you really are; it often removes the illusions; it often sets you free from those old, auto-pilot ways of responding to situations; it often helps you to release the baggage and the habits that have kept you stuck. It can set you free from those old blocks and fears. Meditation can change your life.

Whatever your reasons for wanting to create a space for meditation in your daily life, it is likely to help you. As little as ten minutes a day, over the next 28 days, will produce a shift that you will be able to feel.

How To Spot Someone Who Meditates Regularly

People who meditate regularly experience less stress, more calm, more happiness and a sense of being present in every moment.

They are less rocked by the tides of their emotions and are more able to easily handle their experience of life.

You can feel it, when you meet them. They are somehow more solid – more grounded – than most people. They're more likely to have a gentle smile on their face and a twinkle in their eye, no matter what is going on around them.

> I'm curious:
>
> Do you know anyone who meditates regularly?
>
> How can you tell?
>
> How differently do they react in times of stress?

Getting Started

What To Expect From The 28 Day Meditation Challenge

I don't want to tell you what to expect over the 28 days of this challenge – the best thing you can do is to expect nothing! Suspend all assumptions. Let go of all expectations. Allow yourself to enjoy the process, without judgement.

However, if you read the daily emails, apply the bits that inspire you and do your daily ten minutes of meditating, you will experience results.

I'll be asking the question, *"what is meditation?"* again at the end of your 28 days. That way, you can find your own answer.

What Are We Going To Do For 28 Days?

What will we be covering over the next four weeks?

It is not my intention to provide and produce the world's definitive guide to meditation and then force you to read it!

That's not what you need right now, as you set off on your meditation journey.

However, as a meditation teacher and an NLP trainer, my aim over the 28 days is to provide a kick-start for you, building the foundations of an effective, daily meditation practice. It will help you to get started with your meditation journey - or to re-start it.

Overcoming the common hurdles, creating a little piece of calm in your day and, if you enjoy it, moving on to longer meditation periods, are the aims of the next few weeks.

Once you have completed the 28 days, you will be in a strong position to take your meditation journey wherever you want it to go!

Getting Started

Four Types Of Meditation

We will be covering four types of meditation over the four weeks, to give you an experience of how different people like to meditate; at least one of them will resonate for you.

Often, if people have tried meditation in the past and given up, it's because they were trying a kind of meditation that didn't work for them. So each week you'll get a new meditation to experience. All your meditations are on the MP3s (and optional CD) which accompany this book. The transcripts are in Appendix A, in case you want to record your own version.

There is also a bonus 23 minute deep relaxation. I'll be explaining why deep relaxation can be the key to making meditation work, later in the course.

You don't have to use these audios if you don't want to. You can do a meditation of your own, if you like. But I invite you, just for four weeks, to go with the process and see what happens.

Daily Messages

This book includes daily messages, to help keep you on track.

- Sometimes they'll be 'how to' messages, teaching core meditation and mindfulness techniques
- Sometimes they'll be motivational
- Sometimes they'll be applying psychology and common sense to help you overcome barriers that have been faced by thousands, if not millions, of meditation students across the world
- Sometimes there will be a bit of a 'butt kick', in case you have lapsed, to help you get back on track and commit yourself to carving out ten minutes a day for your meditation time!

The messages are contain essential techniques and inspirational,

Getting Started

potentially life-changing messages, but are also quick to read.

Some days there will be an optional exercise for you to do, if that day's message resonates for you and you want to go deeper. It is up to you; nobody is going to be checking up on you.

Many students of the 28 Day Meditation Challenge have found that reading the daily message at the same time each day helps them to get into the routine of it and makes it easier to remember to do it.

What matters most is that you read each message, in order. If you get behind, just pick up where you left off, rather than jumping ahead. The 28 Day Meditation Challenge helps you to build your foundations, layer by layer. It is important to allow the process to work for you.

If you apply what inspires you from the messages and do your daily meditation, most days, you'll get amazing results. If you don't read the messages and don't do the meditations, then you won't!

I know that sounds obvious, but you might be surprised how often we expect a book to change our life, by leaving it on the bookshelf…

What Do I Need For The 28 Day Meditation Challenge?

What equipment will you need?

- A chair.
- A CD player or MP3 player.

That's it.

We won't be meditating lying down – that's a better posture for deep relaxation and it's also the position we choose for falling asleep. It doesn't help with the 'awake' and 'alert' bit needed for meditating.

Getting Started

One of the key things with meditation, as we will discuss in some of the daily messages, is posture.

Meditation is not about turning your legs into a pretzel and it's not about being uncomfortable.

Good posture can make all the difference for your meditation practice.

Note: we'll be covering good meditation posture at various points over the 28 days.

As optional extras, you might want:

- Headphones. Sometimes it's nice to cocoon yourself in the sound of the meditation.
- You might want extra cushions and even a few sturdy books under your feet, if that helps you with your posture.
- You might want to wrap something around your shoulders, as you meditate.

Sometimes when we sit still, relax and meditate our body can cool down, so having a shawl or a blanket wrapped around your shoulders can help. It is also a way of giving your unconscious mind a signal of *"I am now in my meditating zone - and I want my Monkey Mind to relax and let me do this."*

What You *Won't* Be Getting Over The 28 Days

Before we go any further it is worth me mentioning what you won't be getting from the 28 Day Meditation Challenge.

Elevator Music

The first thing that you won't be getting is tinkly music in the background of the meditations on your CD / MP3s. Here's why: **music can distract you.**

Getting Started

> *I found, over the years, that most of the 'meditations' I had listened to had music in the background. It took 20 years of doing these before I realised, when I started training to become a meditation teacher, that I had never actually meditated before!*
> *I had never really reached that still point.*
> *I had done some amazing deep relaxations and guided visualisations, but I had never actually got to that silent space of peaceful quiet and calm.*

And to be honest, it's tough to get there with 'elevator music' in the background.

The music – though often beautiful - is a way of distracting our mind. It can turn our meditation into a guided deep relaxation instead. It encourages us to focus on hearing the music, rather than moving towards stillness. It encourages us to disappear into a daydream, rather than hearing the instructions, remaining alert and concentrating on doing the specific meditation techniques.

So don't be surprised to hear periods of silence on the meditation audios. This may be a new experience for you. If it feels strange for you, here's a bonus article that might help:

"Why Are We So Scared Of Silence?"

www.28DayMeditationChallenge.com/bonus

Deep Relaxation

What is the difference between meditation and deep relaxation?

A deep relaxation is about relaxing the body and mind - and re-energising. Meditation is about being awake - alert - focusing and concentrating, in order to reach a sense of stillness and wellbeing. Often, the real insights that arrive from meditation happen during the stillness. How can I ask you to quieten your mind if I am playing music in the background?!

Getting Started

There is nothing wrong with background music, but it can be a real distraction from the process of meditating.

Those of you who are used to doing deep relaxations and guided meditations with background music might find it a little disconcerting, sitting in silence. And that's ok!

Sitting in silence is something many of us find challenging. That's why we tend to drown out the silence with TV and radio on in the background all day.

My invitation to you is just to suspend how you would normally react to this quiet time, for ten minutes a day. You never know, it could make a huge difference for you.

A New Religion

The next thing that you won't be getting is a new religion.

There are no required beliefs or thought systems, religious practices or spiritual ideas you have to suddenly adopt to enjoy and benefit from this course.

You don't have to take on any new beliefs to be able to meditate.

Pretty much every spiritual tradition in the world includes meditation, in some form, whether it's prayer, silent sitting, some kind of ritual or even sequences of movement like Tai Chi.

Meditation can be about sitting still or it can be about consciously moving. Mindfulness meditation can even happen while you're doing the washing up, going for a walk or drinking a cup of tea!

The idea behind the 28 Day Meditation Challenge is that it's accessible and open to everyone.

Getting Started

> *Although meditation has the power to change your life, you don't have to change your life to meditate.*

Whatever you believe, if you are able to sit still in a relaxed and alert way, you can be guided through a simple meditation process that will help you de-stress, gently quieten your mind and reach a place of inner calm.

Meditation is a really a natural thing to do, as part of your journey towards happiness, and your meditation practice doesn't care what you believe!

Meditation is a personal thing and I hope that the next 28 days will help you discover how to let it work for you.

> *Don't force it. Don't push it. Don't try too hard. Just do it and let the process help you get the results you're looking for.*

Judgement

Another thing you won't be getting during the four weeks is judgement; this is not a competition, not even with yourself.

Some days your meditation might feel great; other days you might wonder, *"Why did I do that?"*

If your meditation goes well one day but not the next, the only person that needs to know is you. Nobody is going to be sitting there telling you off. It's ok. It's part of the process. There is no critique here. There is no feedback or appraisal. You won't be judged; you won't be scored. You can't get it wrong!

If you find you're judging yourself, please just laugh and let it go.

Expectations

Having expectations of yourself, or your meditation experiences,

Getting Started

can be the biggest barrier to successful meditation.

If you find you're criticising yourself and thinking, "*I am rubbish at meditation,*" because a day's practice didn't go as you had expected - believe me, we have all been there and it's not true – just smile and move on.

> *Meditation is a skill that needs gentle, consistent practice.*

Some days it will go really well some days it may not. It doesn't matter. What matters is your consistency and that you let go and trust the process; trust that your inner wisdom will guide you, if you need to make adaptations to the practices.

Please don't judge yourself! You won't be getting judged in the daily messages and judging yourself is the least useful thing you can do when you are learning how to meditate – or learning any other skill.

What To Do If You Miss A Day?

If you miss a day, please don't beat yourself up. I'm not encouraging you to miss days – seeing results from meditation is about regular practice - but it's not a disaster if a day slips by and you didn't get to meditate. If you get to the end of the day and realise that you haven't done your meditation, sit down and do it.

Acceptance is one of the keys of meditation, as we'll discuss over the coming weeks.

This 28 Day Meditation Challenge is about creating a new habit, in a positive, enjoyable and sustainable way. The worst (and most painful) way to create a new habit is to punish yourself if you don't get it right first time. We work much better with encouragement than with criticism. If you miss a day, just pick your practice up

Getting Started

again, as soon as you realise.

However, it is worth spending a few moments looking at the day you missed:

What was it that caused you to miss a day?

- Did something come up? Did your meditation get de-prioritised because something else was more important? You could take a moment to reflect: was it really more important?
- What could you change about your response to mean that today you do get time to meditate?
- Maybe you need to change the time of day you are meditating? Perhaps trying to fit it in at a time when interruptions are common isn't going to work for you?
- Did you forget why it was that you wanted to meditate? We will be covering that in the next section, on page 36.
- Was it that something got in the way? What could you change today to make that less likely to happen again?
- Sometimes we forget. How could you remind yourself today?

If you miss a day it can actually be useful, because it helps you work out what your unconscious blocks (or excuses!) might be.

Maybe you need to change the time of day that you are meditating? Maybe you need to ask your family for more support? Maybe you need to delegate something?

You'll know what it is that caused you to miss that day. Looking at what it was, without getting defensive or judging yourself, sets you free to take action and to do something about it.

Please don't get annoyed with yourself. Meditate today; tomorrow meditate that day; the day after meditate that day. Let go of the idea of 28 days in a row. Don't put yourself under pressure - really let yourself just flow with this and enjoy the process.

Getting Started

How Long Does It Take To Break – Or Make - A Habit?

Are you wondering why the 28 Day Meditation Challenge is 28 days long? It's a question I'm often asked. So here's the answer:

Because the urban myth that it takes 21 days to break a habit isn't true.

Yes, 21 days gives you a great start on creating your new habit, but ask anyone who's done something for 21 days and they'll generally tell you it wasn't quite long enough to establish the new routine; the new rhythm.

The truth is that it's not really about breaking an old habit. It's about creating a new one, so that the old habit is no longer needed.

It's about a choice - a decision. Then the 28 days are simply about nurturing the habits and behaviours needed, to support that choice.

Today's choices create our tomorrow.

Luckily, meditation can quieten our grasshopper mind, helping us to make more conscious choices. So choosing to cultivate the habit of meditating actually helps you to make the choices that make it easier to meditate. Anyone else's head spinning?!

Here's what happened, a few years ago, when I gave up coffee.

As an NLP trainer and someone who is passionate about psychology and 'how people tick', I did my research first. How long does it take to break a habit? It would seem that everyone has a different opinion on this one.

Some experts say it's 21 days. 21 days is almost accepted as fact. Ask someone in the street, "How long does it take to break a habit?" and they'll invariably recite the '21 day' response.

I have even heard experts in the personal development field

Getting Started

claiming it is 7 days. And I've definitely read plenty of opinion that says the real figure is months, not days or weeks. How long is it? How do you know when you've broken a habit?

> *My caffeine habit had risen to 4 mugs a day of freshly brewed "real" coffee and I was feeling exhausted with every caffeine rush and then energy dip. So I duly went through 4 days of detox and spent 21 days "giving up".*
>
> *Actually, a good friend of mine pointed out I "only" managed 20 1/2 days. And maybe that's where I went wrong, because shortly after my first mug in nearly 3 weeks, I was back on daily doses, that then returned to pre-giving-up levels.*

What had gone wrong?

> *At the same time, I made a commitment to myself to get up every morning at 6 to meditate and have some time for myself, before the family's day began. After just 3 days I found myself actively looking forward to my new habit.*
>
> *And I still remember when I was young that my mum went to a hypnotherapist to give up smoking – but he told her she had already given up the moment she walked through his door. He could tell she had a made a commitment to herself to quit and, 30+ years on, she's never touched a cigarette since.*

I have seen cases such as these, repeatedly, in my work with one-to-one mentoring clients.

So how long does it take to break an old habit or start a new one?

My conclusion, after more than a decade as an NLP Trainer?

It's instant.
*Breaking an old habit or starting a new one is "done" as soon as you make the decision; as soon as you **make a true commitment to yourself** that it's what you're going to do.*

Getting Started

Why didn't giving up coffee work for me back then? Because I didn't really want to. I was doing it because I felt it was "the right thing to do". So my heart wasn't really in it.

As for getting up early each day, that worked because I really wanted to do it. Those who know me will know how precious a commodity sleep is for me(!). But I know how much more centred and chilled out I feel when I've taken that time each morning. So some days I'll get up to meditate and then go back to bed afterwards!

Once you have reached that point, it almost becomes easy, because:
- You have made the decision to do it.
- You know why you're doing it.
- You can feel the benefit.
- If you're 'not in the mood', all you need to do is to imagine how your day will feel if you don't do it. This will normally give you the kick up the butt you need to get on and do it!

So you can break a habit in as little time as it takes you to make a decision.

Yes, after the decision willpower and action are still needed. But it's the strength of that decision – *why* it is important to you – that will make the difference between success and failure.

And that's why it's really important to understand why you want to do the 28 Day Meditation Challenge. Your 'why' will keep you motivated, day by day.

So… why are you doing this?

Let's find out.

Getting Started
The Secret To Keeping Yourself Motivated

Before we start any journey - any challenge - any change - it is really important to know why we are doing it.

Knowing our 'why' - what is motivating us - helps keep us going.

So, before you start, I invite you to take a few moments to do the following exercise.

> Grab yourself a piece of paper and something to write with and allow yourself five or ten minutes just to think and write down your answers to these questions:
>
> 1. Why have you signed up for the 28 Day Meditation Challenge?
>
> 2. What do you hope that meditating every day for ten minutes is going to do for you?
>
> 3. How are you going to notice that it is working for you? Which behaviours, which signs, which emotions are you going to be tracking to feel the progress you are making?
>
> 4. What kinds of barriers can you foresee already that might get in the way of you finding ten minutes a day?
>
> 5. Before you even start this challenge, what are you going to do about those barriers?
>
> 6. What time of day do you think might work best for you?
>
> 7. Do you need to clear anything out of your schedule? Or ask for help? Or delegate something to create that time, ten minutes a day?
>
> Continues on next page…

Getting Started

> And let the answer to this next question bubble up gently for you – don't rationalise it. Complete the following sentence: I choose to meditate for ten minutes a day because…
>
> 8. And when you are ready, write that whole sentence up somewhere. Pin it up around your home or around your office.
>
> 9. If you notice distractions getting in the way of your meditation during the 28 days, you can remind yourself:
>
> *I choose to meditate for ten minutes a day because……*
>
> You might be surprised how often that allows you to prioritise your meditation over the distractions.
>
> 10. And finally, decide when and where you are going to meditate each day.

It can really help to choose a particular place to meditate, because you will be anchoring your body into the habit of remembering that you are about to sit down; you are about to relax; you are about to meditate; you are taking time for yourself.

And, if you can, choosing the same time each day will condition you to expect to meditate. That makes it so much easier to create the habit.

Getting Started

> *If you need to get support to clear time, now is the time to do it, before you start the challenge. Tell your family: "I choose to meditate for ten minutes a day because..."*

The word 'because', as we will be discussing during some of the daily messages, has an amazing power to get people to listen to your request and to help you. When they understand why you want their help and why you want them to support you, it makes it much easier for them to buy in. You might be surprised how much friends, family and co-workers do want to support you. Some of them might even want to join in the 28 Day Challenge with you.

The key is to decide when you are going to meditate, where and what you need to clear out of the way to allow you to do that, and to remember why you're bothering.

Keep A Journal

You might want to keep a journal during the 28 days. This means scribbling down your thoughts, as they come to you, each day – noting what you have learned and experienced.

Sometimes people give up on learning to meditate because they're not seeing results – but results take time... and sometimes we're too busy to notice the progress we're making. We wouldn't expect to buy a pair of running shoes and suddenly be in the Olympics a week later!

> *Meditation is a skill, just like any other we choose to develop. It takes practice. We often don't notice the improvements we have made and the changes that it has brought to our life until we re-read things that we wrote in our journal several weeks or months before.*

Getting Started

So you might want to get yourself a notebook and a pen and spend some time each day - or every few days - writing down what your experiences have been; any suggestions; any insights. Keeping a journal is a useful practice for marking the progress you are making on your journey. It can make a huge difference to your motivation.

Summary

How about filling in your answers to the following questions, as a useful reminder?

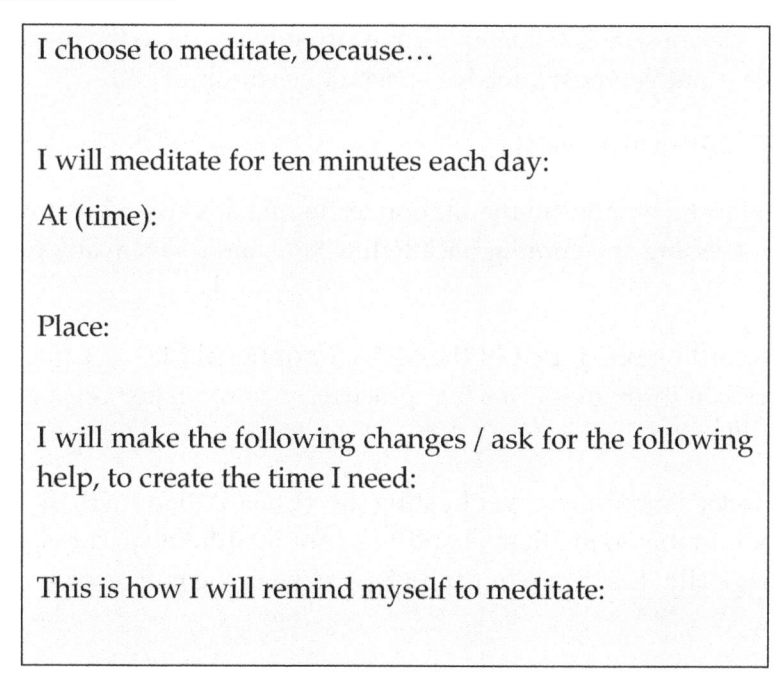

> I choose to meditate, because…
>
> I will meditate for ten minutes each day:
>
> At (time):
>
> Place:
>
> I will make the following changes / ask for the following help, to create the time I need:
>
> This is how I will remind myself to meditate:

That's all for now. I look forward to catching up with you with the Day 1 message and I really, really hope that you enjoy the 28 Day Meditation Challenge.

I hope that it really helps you make subtle shifts in your life, so you can feel calmer, happier and healthier – and whatever else it is that you are aiming for with this challenge.

Week One

Welcome to week one!

This week we will be laying the foundations for your meditation and mindfulness practice.

Your week one meditation gets you started with one of the most simple – and yet most effective – techniques around:

> Breath awareness

It's not just a wonderful meditation technique, it's also a great way of de-stressing and coming back to the 'here and now', at any time of day.

The recording on Track 1 of the MP3s (or optional CD – see page 13) guides you through this ancient practice, so you can just relax and enjoy it!

This week's messages cover busting the #1 meditation myth, how to sit comfortably to meditate, handling your meditation excuses, how to 'magically' find more time and how to keep the momentum going.

I really hope you enjoy your first week.

Namaste,

Clare ♡

DAY 1

BUSTING THE #1 MYTH

Why there's more to meditating than shutting up your Monkey Mind.

Day 1

Day 1: Busting The Number One Meditation Myth

Welcome to the first day of your 28 Day Meditation challenge.

I thought it might be good to begin by dispelling the number one meditation myth. It's the top objection I hear from people when we talk about meditation:

"But I can't shut up my mind!"

There are different ways of saying it:

- I don't have an off switch.
- My mind is too chattering.
- My mind multi-tasks.
- How on earth can I meditate, if I can't make my mind go quiet?
- As soon as I sit still, my mind takes over.

Well, it's a myth. And it's an excuse we often use, to get out of 'having to' meditate. But:

You don't have to shut up your mind and stop thinking to be able to meditate.

Many expert meditators can't do that yet. Some people find it easy. But the fact is that most of us have got Monkey Minds or grasshopper minds, leaping from one thing to the next. And there's more to meditation than an empty mind.

You don't have to make your mind go silent to be able to benefit from meditation.

If that's what you're aiming for, you're likely to be disappointed. Just think about how many decades your mind has been taught to chatter. Yes, you can quieten your thoughts and slow things down using the simple techniques that we'll be covering during the next

Day 1

four weeks. But if you're aiming for total 'mind-silence', then you're setting yourself an extremely high standard to reach.

One of the keys to meditating well – or enjoying mindfulness practice – is to accept your mind. It's about setting yourself free from being attached to your thoughts, letting go of fighting them, so you are better placed to choose thoughts that create inner peace and happiness, rather than stress and anger. You don't need to shut up your mind, to be able to meditate.

In fact:

> *Meditation is a process that helps you to quieten your mind, so it is really the other way round!*

Myth busted?

Strange though it may seem, having a Monkey Mind that chatters can actually be a bonus when you are first starting meditation, because you will quickly notice how ten minutes a day of meditation can help quieten your mind. It takes dedication and it takes practice, just like any skill, but you will see results, even in the next 28 days.

So how on earth are you supposed to meditate with your mind racing?

Simple - there are **three keys to meditation.**

1. **The first one is relaxation.**

    You can't meditate if you're feeling exhausted and stressed. It's a simple fact that when we are tired and stressed we are running on adrenalin - and meditation is about creating a sense of calm.

    You can't do that if you're in your 'fight or flight' stress mode.

Day 1

That's why you'll notice that, at the beginning of each meditation audio, there is a sequence that allows you to settle in the moment; to settle in your body and to start to relax.

It is critical that you let go and do that.

By the way, if you find over the 28 days that it's really hard to sit still, then what you actually need is deep relaxation, not meditation. And we will be covering that in some of the daily messages.

There's a bonus 23 minute deep relaxation on the MP3s (and optional CD) which accompany this book.

2. **The second key is acceptance.**

Your mind will wander: it will think about the shopping; it will think about the ironing; it will think about the school run; it will think about anything it can, because it is used to doing that.

That's the job that it has had for so many years.

Don't judge it; don't dive into a story complaining to it about it getting in the way of your meditation, because suddenly your ten minutes will be over. And you're likely to feel that you wasted your time.

Don't give up if your mind distracts you. Just gently bring yourself back to whatever it is that you are focusing on in that day's meditation.

Learning to accept the Monkey Mind is one of the most amazing ways to de-stress and calm down. It makes a huge difference to your meditation and mindfulness journey. It takes practice, but it is achievable.

The same thing goes for aches and pains, noises and interruptions. With the help of the daily messages and meditation audios, you will be learning how to accept them and not let them get in the way, over the 28 days.

Day 1

3. **The third key to meditation is concentration and focus.**

    You'll be learning how to concentrate and focus on just one thing at a time, to deepen your meditation.

    In our multi-tasking life that can feel like a real challenge - and our conscious mind might give us all sorts of reasons why we can't do it. The key is to choose whether or not you want to buy into those reasons - or whether you want to allow the process of practising meditation to help you make changes in your life.

    If you want to learn to meditate and gain all of the amazing benefits that come with it, it's a choice worth making.

    Over the next 28 days, with just ten minutes of commitment each day, you will notice the difference that meditation and mindfulness can make to your concentration levels and your ability to focus, in all areas of your life.

Help Is At Hand

During the daily messages I will be sharing insider secrets and ancient techniques to help you discover:

- how to deal with thoughts getting in the way
- how to calm and quieten your mind
- how to allow your mind to relax
- and how to accept those thoughts

So you see, meditation is not about switching off your Monkey Mind. But if that's what you want to do, it teaches you how. Meditation is about learning to get your mind to work with you – gently training it - and that can even be quite fun.

Tomorrow we will be looking at how to sit comfortably to meditate - and believe me, it makes all the difference! Meditating doesn't have to hurt!

Day 1

> Yes, you have a monkey mind.
>
> Meditation isn't about switching it off. But it can teach you how, if that's what you want.

Your First Meditation

I have recorded versions of each of the four meditations from the 28 Day Meditation Challenge for you, as well as a bonus 23 minute deep relaxation.

See page 13 for the link to download your MP3 recording or order the optional CD.

This week's meditation is Track 1 of these recordings. *The transcript for your first meditation is in Appendix A, if you'd like to record your own version.* To download MP3 versions (free of charge) please go to:

www.28DayMeditationChallenge.com/bonus

Day 1

Find somewhere quiet; turn off your phone; sit calmly; close your eyes; relax and enjoy the beginning of your 28 Day Meditation Challenge.

Namaste,

Clare

P. S. Tomorrow we'll be looking at the foundations of good meditation posture, which is key to helping you to relax, concentrate and enjoy your meditation practice.

For today, follow the instructions on the meditation audio, to help you get used to the process without worrying about how you're sitting.

Day 1 Affirmation

I choose to enjoy today's meditation.

DAY 2

ARE YOU SITTING COMFORTABLY?

Insider secrets that make meditating less painful!

Day 2: Are You Sitting Comfortably?

One of the most common objections I hear when talking to people about meditation is that they can't sit still for that long; it makes their legs hurt and their back ache.

We live in a society where being busy and multi-tasking are badges of honour that we wear with pride. The idea of sitting still and doing nothing can be a real shocker.

As you'll remember from yesterday, one of the keys to enjoying meditation is acceptance:

- accepting your surroundings
- accepting your mind
- accepting your emotions
- accepting your body
- accepting your breathing

But if meditation hurts, it's worth getting advice on your posture.

Meditation isn't meant to hurt!

It's not about turning your legs into a pretzel.

In fact one of the best places to do meditation, when you are starting out, is on a chair, rather than on the floor.

But many of us find it uncomfortable to sit still.

Why is that?

Often it is down to tension.

It might be physical tension in the body or it might be due to stress, which is effectively mental tension.

It can also be caused by tiredness – it takes energy to sit still – in which case a deep relaxation will help.

Day 2

How Should You Sit To Meditate?

We often think we have to sit in a particular way to meditate, conjuring up images of über-serene models or gnarled yogis, with their legs contorted into the lotus position. Yes, certain traditions have their 'usual' postures. But if they don't work for you, that's ok. There's no such thing as 'should' or 'have to', when it comes to getting meditation to work for you.

> *I have a wonderful, inspirational friend who is in her eighties. We studied together to become meditation teachers. She suffers from genuine physical pain when she sits, and it can take her over an hour to get her body moving in the mornings.*
> *But despite all that, she is still able to find a way to sit still and meditate. I figure that if she can do it, there's no way I'm entitled to any excuses!*

But sitting still for ten minutes is perfectly achievable - think about a typical day:

- when we are driving, we sit for more than ten minutes
- when we are at work, we manage
- at mealtimes, most of us do it
- watching television, we can sit for hours
- on Facebook... well... 'nuff said!

So we know we can sit still for ten minutes.

But there is something about meditation that can make us tense up into an artificial sitting position.

The most important way to sit when you are meditating is in a way that allows you to feel comfortable, but awake, to make it easy to accept your body. Sometimes if, at a deeper level, we are resisting our meditation, it can make our body tense up, causing discomfort and physical pain – all caused by mental tension.

Day 2

What To Do If Meditating Hurts

The first tactic in dealing with meditation pain is to notice whether it is 'real pain' or 'give me attention' pain.

Is It 'Pretend Pain'?

If you make a slight movement of the bit of you that is aching, does the pain go away? Yes? Then it's most likely 'give me attention' pain - your Monkey Mind trying to distract you from your meditation. And that's ok!

In that case, here's a solution:

> *Imagine you're breathing into the area that feels tense.*
> *As you breathe in, imagine filling that area with a soft, golden light.*
> *As you breathe out, imagine the tension and discomfort melting away, allowing the area to relax.*
> *Do that for three breaths and the discomfort almost always goes.*

Even the simple action of renaming this 'pain' as 'discomfort' takes away its potency.

If it's 'real' pain...

If pain doesn't go away when you make a small movement, then it's 'legitimate' or 'real' pain. Don't ignore it! Change your position. If it happens regularly, ask for help with your posture. A good meditation teacher, chiropractor, osteopath or physiotherapist should be able to help.

What About 'Pins & Needles'?

This is a really common problem for meditators. If a part of your body has its blood flow restricted, the familiar sensation of 'pins and needles' will be the result.

Day 2

If you get this during your meditation, don't be a martyr. Change your position, let the blood flow return and then go back to meditating. If it happens regularly, then you need to revisit the posture advice in today's message and in the 'Getting Started' section. If you are really stuck, then ask for help with your meditation posture, as for the 'real pain' advice.

> Meditation isn't supposed to hurt.
>
> It's about finding that space where your body meets your spirit.
>
> It's not about turning your legs into a pretzel.

Good Posture Is Key

Sitting with good posture is key to enjoying your meditation.

> *Meditation isn't supposed to hurt. It's not about turning your legs into a pretzel.*

Day 2

If you're sitting on a chair, it is important to have your back quite straight, rather than slouching. You want to be feeling relaxed, but alert. The easiest way to achieve this is to have the parasympathetic and sympathetic nervous systems in balance. The parasympathetic nervous system is about relaxation, the sympathetic nervous system is about the body's stress response.

To get them in balance, hold your back quite straight, with a slight tension at the midpoint. This activates both the nervous systems and helps to bring them into balance, leaving you relaxed, but alert.

That's why we don't meditate lying down - lying down is how we fall asleep.

Poor back posture during meditation can make you feel breathless. If your back is curved and your belly is squashed, your diaphragm will struggle to work properly and your lungs will also be squashed. This can impact the oxygen levels in the blood stream, which can trigger the uncomfortable feeling of breathlessness, which becomes more obvious when you're sitting still and silently during meditation.

If you notice yourself feeling breathless, you might like to take 3 deep, sighing breaths - as we do at the beginning of each meditation - and to stretch your back gently. This should sort things. It's also worth checking you're not holding your breath - easy to do when you're concentrating!

Note: persistent breathlessness should not be ignored – go and get appropriate medical help!

What Does Good Posture Feel Like?

To get a sense of what good meditation posture feels like:
- Imagine a string is connected to the crown of your head.
- Imagine someone is gently pulling that string, to help you

Day 2

      lengthen your spine, from the base all the way up to your neck.

- Then tuck your chin slightly in - you'll feel your neck lengthening and your jaw relaxing.
- Make sure your shoulders aren't around your ears, but are feeling relaxed.
- It also really helps to have your hips either level or slightly above your knees, to prevent stress in the knee joints and to help you keep your back straight.

There you go!

This might feel a little strange at first, but it can really help with your meditation practice.

The key to good meditation posture is stability.

A stable posture allows your body – and mind – to relax. Once you are used to it, it takes very little effort to maintain it, allowing you to get on with your meditation.

How To Make Meditation More Comfortable

Playing with this at regular points during your day, when you're not meditating, will help your body get used to relaxing into this posture – as well as gently strengthening your back muscles. Improving your posture generally during the day will make a big difference. Good posture releases tension and strengthens the muscles you use during seated meditation practice.

When you're meditating in a chair, you might want to:

- add a cushion, just under your pelvis, to tilt it slightly forwards.

Day 2

If you are like me, with shorter legs, you might want to:

- add something under your feet, so that your thighs can be level, your back relaxed and your feet firmly resting on something. Dangling feet and meditation don't go well together. I often use the phonebook, but you could use a cushion or a rolled up blanket.

If you have the opposite problem - long legs - then you might like to:

- use a cushion under your bottom, to raise yourself up, so that your knees aren't pointing towards the ceiling.

The key is to have your pelvis level with your knees – not above or below them.

Get Help With Your Posture

Good posture is a really important part of being able to meditate.

There are many tips, techniques and insider secrets, to make sitting still easier - especially when you start doing longer meditations.

But for now, how about sharing your questions?

How is your body reacting to sitting still for 10 minutes?

How are you handling it?

Got any advice you'd like to share? Or perhaps you'd like some clarity, to check what you're doing is working?

How about visiting the 28 Day Meditation Challenge's Facebook page and sharing your thoughts on this? If you'd like feedback on your posture, you could even upload a photo.

www.facebook.com/28DayMeditationChallengeCourse

Day 2

Long-Term Solutions

Longer term, if you are finding meditation uncomfortable, you might want to consider chiropractic or osteopathy treatment, or consulting a posture expert, to correct any structural problems and to give you exercises to strengthen your back muscles.

If you really find you can't sit still, for physiological reasons, don't worry. There are other types of meditation, such as mindfulness, that you can easily practice while you are moving around. We will be covering those in week three.

Posture Videos and Tutorials

Please make sure you have registered for this book's bonuses and you'll be able to get your hands on the latest videos and tutorials on good meditation posture.

I'll also be sharing them via the book's Facebook page. It's a great place to get answers to your meditation posture questions.

www.Facebook.com/28DayMeditationChallengeCourse

Aside: It's not uncommon for people to find it hard to get started, when they're beginning a new habit, such as meditating for ten minutes a day.

If that resonates for you, there's a bonus article, which shares how others have handled it and made a start:

"Why Do We Find It So Hard To Get Started?"
Appendix B

Day 2

I hope you really enjoy today's meditation!

Namaste,

Clare

P. S. Tomorrow we're going to be discovering the key to breaking free from your meditation excuses.

P. P. S. Each day has an image, with a key quote. **All of these are available for you to download, free of charge**, to print out and use around your home, if they inspire you. You could even share them with your friends. They're available at the bonus link.

www.28DayMeditationChallenge.com/bonus

Day 2 Affirmation

I choose a comfortable position, to help me meditate.

DAY 3

WHAT ARE YOUR FAVOURITE EXCUSES?

Discover the key to breaking free from your meditation excuses.

Day 3: What Are Your Favourite Meditation Excuses?

We've all got them - the reasons why we can't meditate - our meditation excuses:

- *I don't have time*
- *I'm too tired*
- *there is too much to do*
- *it doesn't work for me*
- *it's boring…*

We may have spent years, believing in them… But…

> *What if we could see meditation as a solution, instead of a 'chore' to fit in?*

Meditation can help us to enjoy life more, feel less stressed and get more done, rather than being an obligation that takes up valuable time.

It's said that meditation and prayer for example are two sides of the same coin. There's a lovely story about Archbishop Desmond Tutu on finding time to meditate or pray:

> *Archbishop Desmond Tutu was asked by a journalist how long he prays for each day. He is busy jetting around the world, and no doubt the journalist was trying to catch him out with this question. But his answer was: "I am so busy, if I want to get everything done I cannot pray for less than two hours a day!"*

I remember reading that article; it stopped me in my tracks. I'm guessing that, although I often feel really busy, someone like Desmond Tutu might just be a bit busier than me. And he says he can't get it all done without meditative prayer space. It was time to review my excuses!

Day 3

We all have them - our favourite excuses (sorry - totally valid reasons!) why we don't meditate. They might be about time, about energy, about being tired, about having too much to do, about not knowing how... or perhaps you're more creative than that!

Quick Exercise:

Day 3 of your 28 Day Meditation Challenge is a really good time to look at your excuses.

- What are your excuses for not meditating?
- What have they been in the past?
- What are they today?
- What are you going to do about them?
- And when?!

Not sure what your excuses are? Here's a simple question to help you uncover them:

"I can't meditate today, because..."

The answer to that question holds the secret to discovering – and then being able to sort out – your meditation excuses.

I'm curious: what are your favourite excuses for not meditating? How about sharing them with others via the Facebook page:

www.Facebook.com/28DayMeditationChallengeCourse

The Key To Breaking Free From Your Meditation Excuses?

If you find your excuses are still coming up for you over the 28 days, it's worth going back to the 'Getting Started' section and reviewing the Secret To Keeping Yourself Motivated' exercise. It's on page 36.

Day 3

Often, when we remember *why* we want to do something, it helps our excuses effortlessly disappear. In fact, it's such a magic formula for life in general, that I'll say it again:

*When we are truly convinced about **why** we want to do something, our excuses for not doing it can effortlessly disappear.*

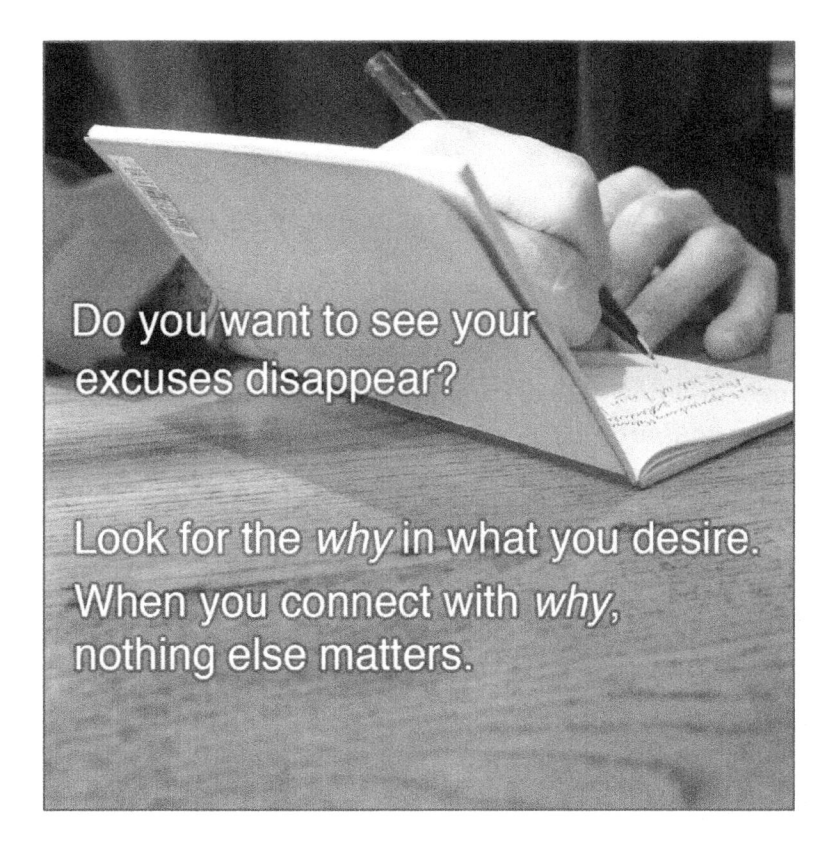

> Do you want to see your excuses disappear?
>
> Look for the *why* in what you desire. When you connect with *why*, nothing else matters.

Over the 28 days, these messages will be covering many of our common excuses, to help you find your own solutions.

Sometimes the best solution is, as the sportswear manufacturer said:

"Just do it!"

It's easy to spend more time complaining to ourselves about our

Day 3

excuse than the ten minutes that your meditation would have taken…

If we know *why* we want to do something, then excuses like "*I don't feel like it*," or "*I'm not in the mood*," tend to melt away. And we feel better afterwards!

Those ten minutes can have a positive impact on the whole of your day.

So I really hope you enjoy today's meditation.

Namaste,

Clare

P. S. Tomorrow we're going to be dealing with the #1 meditation excuse, once and for all!

P. P. S. How are you getting on with your meditation posture? If you'd like to know more about how to have good meditation posture – and how to feel comfortable about meditating on a chair, there's a bonus article:

"5 Things You Need To Know About Meditating on A Chair"

Appendix B

Day 3 Affirmation

I remember why I want to meditate. I choose to do it.

DAY 4

BUT I DON'T HAVE TIME TO MEDITATE!

Dealing with the #1 meditation excuse, once and for all!

Day 4

Day 4: But I Don't Have Time To Meditate!

How have the first few days been going? Have you managed to meditate yet? I really hope you're enjoying the beginning of your 28 Day Meditation Challenge. Today we're talking about **how to find time to meditate**.

This is one of the most common reasons I hear from people about why they don't meditate... and I have to confess that I have lost count of how often I have used it myself!

> *Someone I was talking to recently about this course was raving about wanting to learn how to meditate. And she was excited about the idea of being able to lay the foundations, day by day, in the comfort of her own home, through the 28 Day Meditation Challenge.*
> *But when I asked her if she could spare ten minutes a day for it, her answer was, "No! I'm way too busy!" She was so convinced by her excuse that there was no room left for change.*

Is it really true that our lives are too full to find time to meditate?

It is true that we often *believe* that we don't have time to meditate. But there's a difference between truth and belief.

We believe our stories and excuses, telling them to ourselves so often that they become a pseudo-truth that we no longer question – like 'received wisdom'. We even start to believe in other people's excuses! But is it really true?

It's funny how, for example, if we fall in love, we suddenly find plenty of evenings and weekends to spend with that new person:

- we watch less TV
- we read fewer magazines
- we spend less time on chores
- we use our time more intentionally
- we drop anything that's not essential

Day 4

Is it really too much for your mind, body and soul to ask for ten minutes of your time each day for something that can dramatically impact your life?

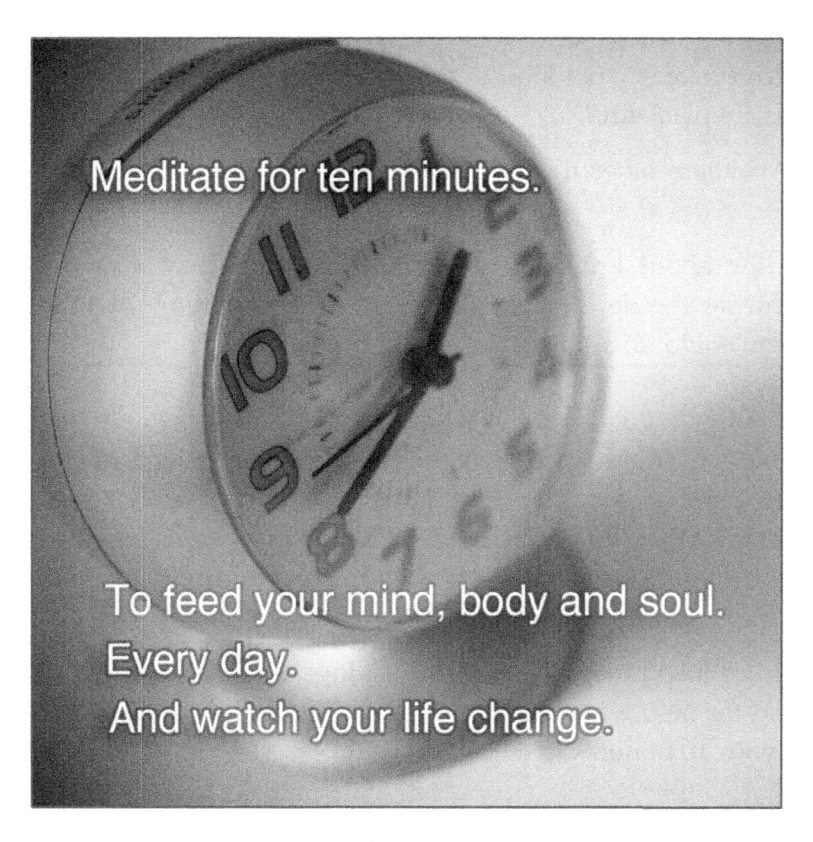

> Meditate for ten minutes.
> To feed your mind, body and soul.
> Every day.
> And watch your life change.

There are many 'important jobs' and distractions during the day that steal our time; things that crop up unexpectedly, where we give them our immediate attention. Everything else falls off the table, including our meditation. Yet if we said to those things, "*I will come back to you later,*" it's amazing how they either go away or take up less time.

The classic example is a phone call.
You're in the middle of something important, but you answer the phone anyway. The conversation takes ten minutes. Then you go

Day 4

back to what you were doing.
You found ten minutes for the interruption.
So why do we find it so hard to find ten minutes to meditate…?

Quick Exercise:

I'm curious: what kind of things do you do in ten minutes in a typical day?

Are there other things that you could let go of, even just for 28 days?

How about brainstorming a list of things that you do during the day that might be wasting your time or that you could do a bit less of? Yes, right now!

Maybe you could watch ten minutes' less television? Maybe you could spend 28 days choosing not to watch the news? Or spend ten minutes less per day on Facebook? Read your emails less often? Or get someone else to do the washing up? Or you could fit meditation in during your lunch break?

Stuck for inspiration? How about asking your friends for ideas and asking for help with your top time wasters? How are you going to find your 10 minutes to meditate today?

Have you got any tips or suggestions that you'd like to share? Want to find out how others are managing it?

How about posting your thoughts on this one on our Facebook page:

www.Facebook.com/28DayMeditationChallengeCourse

What could you let go of or rearrange about your day, to make time for just ten minutes of meditation?

Day 4

Are you filling your time with things to do? It's nearly an epidemic. It's as though we're so scared of 'stopping' and 'being' that we feel guilty about doing nothing.

Not In The Mood To Meditate?

If it's more of a general thing – not being in the mood to meditate – here's a bonus article I've written for you, which might help:

> *"Feeling Down? Why Meditation Could Be Just What You Need"*
>
> www.28DayMeditationChallenge.com/bonus

Pick A Time That Works For You

One of the other key things for making time for meditation is picking a time of day that works for you.

Don't try and fit meditation in when you are already really busy and you know you're prone to interruptions. It might seem common sense, but it's amazing how often we try that one.

> *For example, many people like to meditate first thing in the morning. But mornings can be very busy times, especially if you have to get to work or get the kids to school. To fit in your meditation at that time, either something needs to give, or you'll need to get up earlier…*

What's The 'Best' Time Of Day To Meditate?

There is no right or wrong time of day to do meditation. Yes, there are 'traditional' times (such as early morning / sunrise / 4am!). However, it's more important just to do your meditation, rather than worrying about when someone says you 'should' do it.

The best time is one when you know you have got a bit more

Day 4

control over your time, even if that is last thing at night when everybody else has fallen asleep and you are feeling tired.

> *Personally, life with three young boys can be very busy and I (obviously!) can't leave them unattended while I sit around with my eyes closed, trying not to move... So I usually meditate before the family wakes up in the morning, or just after the boys have gone to sleep, in the evening.*
>
> *Yes, the morning meditation 'costs me' sleep, but that time leaves me feeling much more refreshed and focussed than the extra sleep would have done. It's rare for me to miss my meditation, even at weekends, because it has become a routine, a habit, and I am convinced about why I am doing it. But it still takes dedication!*

There will be a 'best time' for you, in your life, with your schedule and commitments – though it might take a little experimenting to find it.

Avoid meditating after eating.

It's tough to meditate on a full stomach, shortly after eating. Remember: meditation is about concentration, which takes effort and energy. When your body is digesting food, it needs to use its energy for that, so meditation can lead to indigestion or even nausea, especially if you're focussing on your breathing and working your diaphragm! Some foods, such as sugar and wheat, can make us feel tired, so you would be struggling to stay awake and to focus during your meditation.

Later on in the 28 days I will be sharing insider secrets to help you wake yourself up, to meditate - to help with those days when you have to choose a time when you might be feeling tired, or not in the mood.

The fact is that ten minutes really isn't very long... I strongly suspect there are very few of us who genuinely couldn't find time for it, especially if we remember why it is that we are motivated to

Day 4

do it. Go back to the 'Getting Started' section and the 'Secret To Keeping Yourself Motivated' exercise (on page 36), if you need to refresh your memory!

So how are you going to find your ten minutes to meditate today?

I hope you really enjoy today's meditation!

Namaste,

Clare

P. S. Tomorrow we'll be looking at how to get moral support (at home or at work) for your meditation time. It's easier than you might think.

Day 4 Affirmation

I choose to take ten minutes to meditate today.

DAY 5

HOW TO GET MORAL SUPPORT FOR YOUR MEDITATION TIME

Why asking for help could be easier than you might think.

Day 5: How To Get Moral Support For Your Meditation Time

How have the first four days been? Ready to go with day five? Today we're talking moral support.

Sometimes, when we want to start a new habit, the most difficult place to get moral support is at home. Yet it can make all the difference to us when those with whom we spend the most time understand what it is we are trying to achieve - and support us on that journey.

One of the most important ways to get moral support at home (or at work, if that's where you're going to be meditating) is to know *why* you want to meditate.

Yes, we're back to that one again!

> *There was some research, a few years ago, about the impact of telling others why you want to do something.*
> *Psychologists did an experiment in an office. In this study, somebody asked to jump to the front of a long queue for the photocopier. Most of the time the others in the queue said 'no'. In the final experiment, the researchers got the queue jumper to use the word 'because' and then follow it with their reason:*
> *"Please may I jump the queue, because..." and all they said was, "I have some photocopying to do."*
> *Everybody else in the queue had the same reason for standing there (unless they were just chatting!). Yet nearly everybody willingly let the person jump the queue.*
>
> **It shows the power of the word 'because'.**

If you talk to your family and explain *why* you're choosing to spend ten minutes a day meditating, it will be easier for them to support you. They will be much more likely to give you the time and space you need. They are less likely to distract you and are more likely to be actively interested in what you're up to - perhaps even joining in!

Day 5

What is your 'because'?

Knowing your 'because', your 'why' for meditating helps you ask for moral support at home or work.

You might want to explain to your family how meditation is going to help you feel calmer or happier or more relaxed. Whatever your 'why' was back in the 'Getting Started' section on page 36, you can share it with them. It will help them to understand.

Tell them what you need from them.

And as your family starts to see the results of your meditation practice, they're more likely to give their support. For example, one student on the 28 Day Meditation Challenge online course reported:

> *"I have been feeling so chilled out. In fact, I have just been able to quietly talk my husband out of making a very hasty and ill-judged decision, rather than huffing and puffing and telling him he's wrong."*

Her meditation practice was already having noticeable benefits for her family.

Sometimes it can feel difficult to voice our needs - to tell others what help we need. But asking for help is essential, if we want to create a new habit that requires the support of others.

What support do you need at home / at work?

Sometimes, when we want to start a new habit, the most difficult place to get moral support is at home. Yet it can make all the difference to us when those that we spend the most time with understand what it is we are trying to achieve - and support us on that journey.

Perhaps you need people not to interrupt you; not to distract you; to do the washing up after dinner; to respect your choice; to be quiet

Day 5

for ten minutes; to remind you to do it or even to do it with you?

If there is something you need, it's not fair to expect them to guess. You need to tell them!

If this is something that you struggle with, then it is really worth looking into Marshall Rosenberg's inspiring work on Non-Violent Communication. He created processes to help us practise expressing our unmet needs, without creating conflict.

Here's where you can find out more about his work:

www.28DayMeditationChallenge.com/bonus

And if you'd like some more on this, there's an article I have written for you: **"Six Secrets For Training Your Family To Help You Meditate"** at the same link.

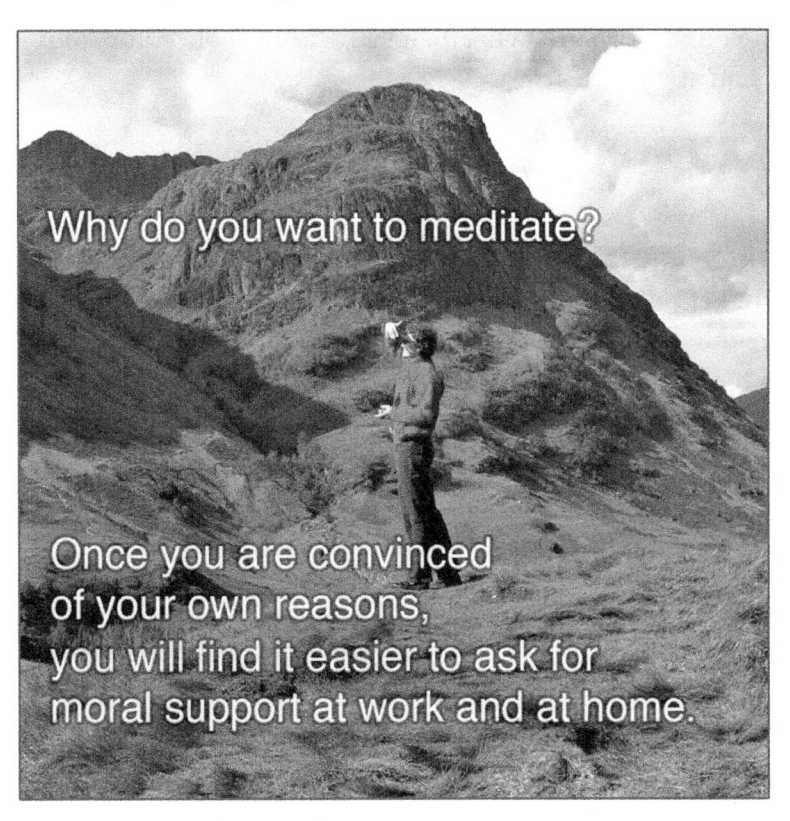

Why do you want to meditate?

Once you are convinced of your own reasons, you will find it easier to ask for moral support at work and at home.

Day 5

Another person on the 28 Day Meditation Challenge online course fed back that:

"After chatting with my husband, he understands how important it is for me to have ME time. Thank you for inspiring me to ask for his help with this. It's been very useful."

Busy mum of young children

It's a common theme from people taking part in the course that people say yes, when they ask them for help to fit in their meditation time.

Not sure what help you need? Here's a simple exercise to uncover those unmet needs.

Quick Exercise:

If you're not sure what help you need, you could look again at your excuses:

"I'd be able to meditate, if only..."

or

"I can't find time to meditate, because..."

The end of the sentence gives clues as to the support you might need.

So my questions for you today are:

What support do you want or need at home to complete the 28 Day Meditation Challenge?

What do you need to do or say to get that support?

How will you know when you have got it?

How about sharing your answers over at our Facebook page?

www.Facebook.com/28DayMeditationChallengeCourse

Day 5

I hope you really enjoy today's meditation!

Namaste,

Clare

P. S. Tomorrow we're going to be talking about what to do if you miss a day... Not that it's an invitation to do so today!

Day 5 Affirmation

I ask for help and support when I need it.

DAY 6

WHAT TO DO IF YOU MISS A DAY

Why beating yourself up is the worst thing you can do.

Day 6: What To Do If You Miss A Day

How was day five? Did you get to meditate yesterday? How are you finding the process, now you're nearly a week in?

Today we're talking about what happens if you miss a day.

Before we start, you might be surprised that no one is going to tell you off if you miss a day. No one is going to get cross. No one is going to shout.

No one is going to hold it against you. No one wants you to feel guilty. Why?

Because you're human! And you're starting out on this 28 day (and hopefully life-long) journey of practising meditation. Whenever we start something new, it's inevitable that every few steps forward could include a pause or even a little step back. And that's ok. The key is to be making regular progress, over time.

> *What's the worst thing you can do if you miss a day?*
> *Beat yourself up about it.*

Why? Because that's exactly what your Monkey Mind wants! It's scared of the silence. It's worried that it won't be important any more, once you know how to manage it. It has already been throwing every excuse imaginable at you, to distract you from meditating. Just imagine how much fun it could get from spending hours, days or weeks telling you how rubbish you are at meditating, just because you missed a day. Then your missed day becomes a missed few days, which become a missed week, weeks, a month, months... and then you've given up.

Is that what you really want?

So I strongly suggest that you accept the fact that you missed a day; don't beat yourself up; don't judge yourself; it happened; it's done; it's in the past; the only person who could undo it is someone with a time machine.

Day 6

They key is to learn from it, then let it go.

By figuring out why you missed a day, you can make it less likely to happen in the future.

- **Perhaps you forgot?**
  Then how will you remind yourself next time? Do you need to set an alarm? Do you need to put a reminder note up somewhere around the house?

- **Were you too busy?**
  Well, what could you let go of, to find ten minutes in your day? Do you need to change the time you are doing your meditation?

- **Did you make an excuse?**
  Perhaps meditation isn't really what you want to do at this stage (dare I say it?!)? Being really honest with yourself, maybe you haven't really chosen to start yet? Or maybe you're a bit scared or nervous or unsure or unclear about what to do and how to do it?

- **Did you need moral support?**
  Remember, if you want to share this journey, then the online version of the 28 Day Meditation Challenge gives you a forum to share your experiences and get answers to your questions: www.28DayMeditationChallenge.com.

  And you can share your experiences at our Facebook Page: www.Facebook.com/28DayMeditationChallengeCourse

- **Perhaps it's a completely different reason?**
  Whatever it is, becoming aware of the cause is the key to choosing whether or not you want to make changes.

Once you figured out how it happened – and what you want to learn from it – let it go.

Day 6

> It's the choice you make right now, here in this moment, which creates your future.

If you'd like some inspiration on how to handle this one, how about sharing your experiences? You could see how others have tackled this and they could give you some tips and inspiration at:

www.Facebook.com/28DayMeditationChallengeCourse

> *There was a famous hypnotherapist called Milton Erickson. He taught people about the power of concentrating on the one single thing that they are doing at that time and not allowing past performance issues to affect their present or their future.*
> *He often worked with Olympic athletes who, for example, might need to perform the same task many times over, but often lost their nerve in the final few rounds.*
> *He once trained an Olympic Shooting Team, who had to shoot at a target twenty times - and who were shooting brilliantly. But by the time they got to the final few shots, as the pressure built up,*

Day 6

> their nerves would kick in and they would fluff the last few targets, just when they were about to win gold. He taught them to focus on 'I take this shot, and then I do it now, and then I do it now'.
>
> He taught them to let go of whatever had gone before, not to worry about what was coming next and simply focus on that one time.

It is the same with our meditation. What has gone before is done.

It is the choice we make right now that creates our future.

So let's get started!

I hope you really enjoy today's meditation!

Namaste,

Clare

P. S. Tomorrow we're going to be talking about how to keep your momentum going.

Day 6 Affirmation

Yesterday has been and gone. It's what I do today that matters.

DAY 7

KEEPING THE MOMENTUM GOING

The hidden secret to creating lasting change.

Day 7

Day 7: Keeping The Momentum Going

Congratulations! You have made it through your first week of the 28 Day Meditation Challenge and that's wonderful news!

I'm curious: how are you getting on?

- How has the first week been? Have you been doing the meditation every day?
- If it has slipped for a day, have you looked at your reasons why? And have you done something about it?
- How is your posture going?
- Have you got the support you need?
- Has your experience of meditating been what you were expecting?
- How are you feeling about taking your daily ten minutes?

Keeping your momentum going

One of the things that can happen at this stage is feeling disillusioned, because the results haven't been instantaneous…

Although the first seven days of the 28 Day Meditation Challenge can help you see tangible shifts, we live in a culture that craves instant results.

Perhaps it's because we have often forgotten (or maybe never learned!) how to apply consistent effort, over time, to get the results we want.

You hear people saying, "*Well, I did it for a while, but then I quit.*"

Whether it's weight loss, getting fit, learning to play an instrument, learning a foreign language or any other skill, it's nearly an epidemic. If we don't get fast results, we're tempted to believe we're failures and give up.

I call it "Gimme now!" syndrome.

Day 7

But it doesn't have to be that way.

There are examples, even in our fast-paced, instant-delivery world, of changes being made by many people who are putting in the effort, consistently, over time, and creating amazing changes in their lives.

> *If you want to watch a video to inspire you to keep going, even if you're finding it tough to create your meditation habit, then here's one you'll definitely want to check out. It's by an inspirational man called Arthur Boorman. I won't say any more – I'll let him tell you himself.*
>
> *http://www.clarejosa.com/?p=1098*

What Can Meditation Learn From The World Of Zumba?

Zumba is a Latin dance-inspired fitness program created by dancer and choreographer Alberto "Beto" Perez in Colombia during the 1990s.

It has taken off in a way that few would have predicted, with many thousands turning up each week to exercise. It seems to bypass our natural excuses and inertia and has many ardent fans. Why is that?

Perhaps because Zumba has accidentally, or maybe deliberately, tapped into some of the best psychological strategies for reducing our resistance to change and keeping us motivated.

Here are seven reasons why Zumba works so well.

1. It's fun
2. There's no judgement
3. You can't get it 'wrong' (ok, not really wrong!)
4. It's open to pretty much everyone - there are no special pre-requisites

Day 7

5. You can do it with friends - so it creates a sense of community

6. It's regular - the classes remind you to come back 'little & often', rather than doing ten classes at once and not being able to move the next day

7. People know the results will build up over time and that a single class won't suddenly give them the body of an athlete!

Does it have to be any different with meditation?

Ok, so I'm not suggesting you leap around the room to Latin American music while you meditate (though that is an option in week 3, when we'll be talking about mindfulness!). But we can apply all of the strategies that make Zumba work so well to our meditation practice, right here, right now.

1. **We can make it fun.**
   Do it with a smile on your face; look forward to it; allow yourself to enjoy it; don't see it as a chore.

2. **There's no judgement.**
   No one else is judging you; it's not a competition; so why on earth judge yourself? (More on this in future messages – and remember day 6's message?)

3. **You can't get it 'wrong'.**
   Honestly! (No matter what meditation teachers may have told you in the past…) Your meditation practice just 'is'. Yes, there are things you can tweak to make it more effective, but there's no 'right' or 'wrong'.

4. **It's open to all.**
   There are no pre-requisites for learning meditation, other than wanting to do it. It doesn't matter how fit you are, how busy you are, what your beliefs are, what your past is. Meditation is there, waiting for you, whenever you decide

Day 7

you're ready.

5. **You can do it with friends.**
   Yes, meditating in a group can be a powerful experience. And that's one of the reasons why we created the peer support forum, as part of the online version of the 28 Day Meditation Challenge course, to help you connect with people - to create a community - so you can enjoy mutual support and get to know others on a similar journey.

   How about roping in some friends to do the 28 Day Meditation Challenge with you? I have even had students meditating together using Skype!

6. **It's regular.**
   Meditating for an hour once a week has much less impact for you than a shorter period, every day. Regular, consistent practise is what produces results.

7. **Results build up over time.**
   Even after the first week, people on the 28 Day Meditation Challenge report that they are noticing the 'ripple effect' of meditation in their daily life – which is wonderful news. Just imagine how it's going to feel after 28 days (or more!).

If, despite all of this, you're still feeling in need of some motivation to keep going, it could be that you're not getting what you were hoping for.

We'll be talking about how our expectations are the biggest enemy of successful meditation later in the 28 days. But for now, it might be worth reviewing what your expectations are from meditation.

Day 7

> *Just like any skill, it takes practice and there really is no such thing as instant results when you are looking at trying to quieten your mind and reach your inner still point.*

Make sure you're open to noticing the changes that are already happening.

And the fact that you've got to 7 days is wonderful! You're creating your new habit. You have made your choice and that gives you huge power and motivation to keep going for the rest of the 28 Day Challenge.

> *Inspiration gives us the idea;*
> *Motivation gets us started;*
> *But it's routine and habit that create change.*

If you'd like some extra inspiration to help you keep going, even if you don't feel like it, then this bonus article is well worth reading.

"How To Meditate, Even When You're Not In The Mood"

www.28DayMeditationChallenge.com/bonus

I hope you really enjoy today's meditation!

Namaste,

Clare

P. S. Tomorrow you're going to get the week 2 meditation - and for the next week, we're going to be dealing with your Monkey Mind!

Day 7

Inspiration gives us the idea;

motivation gets us started;

but it's routine and habit that

create change.

Day 7 Affirmation

I know that each and every meditation takes me a step further on my journey.

Week Two

Welcome to week two!

This week we're moving into the realm of the Monkey Mind.

We'll be discovering some of the tricks it can play and how you can reclaim control, without turning things into a war.

We'll be looking at how to stop others from stealing your meditation time and how to get over an addiction to putting your 'to do' list first.

I'll be sharing the insider secret to fast-track creating any new habit and spilling the beans on how to get past the 'meditation hump'.

Enjoy!

Namaste,

Clare

DAY 8

MAKING FRIENDS WITH YOUR MONKEY MIND

Why this could be the best choice you ever make.

Day 8

Day 8: Making Friends With Your Monkey Mind

Congratulations! You're into week two of your 28 Day Meditation Challenge.

Last week, as you may have spotted, our meditation was all about grounding - getting out of our stressed minds and drawing our awareness back into the physical body, through watching our breathing.

This week we're dealing with that pesky Monkey Mind! So make sure you move on to your week 2 meditation today. It's Track 2 on the MP3s (and optional CD) which accompany this book. To download an MP3 version or order a CD:

www.28DayMeditationChallenge.com/bonus

One of the things I am often asked at this stage is whether you 'should' meditate with your eyes opened or closed. Different traditions have differing viewpoints. I generally suggest that you have your eyes softly closed, so there is no tension in your eye or facial muscles. But, ultimately, enjoying your meditation is about choosing whatever works for you. Most people prefer to meditate with their eyes closed, because it shuts out visual distractions, but it's up to you. Perhaps you would like to try it both ways, to experience the difference?

So, diving into the Monkey Mind…

Many of us find that, as soon as we sit still and quietly, our mind starts to race. It's as though everything it has been trying to say to us all day has to come out at once, because it's finally got our attention. In fact, this is the reason why many of us feel uncomfortable with

Day 8

silence. You can spot this by seeing whether you need to have the radio or television going in the background most of the day.

Actually, the Monkey Mind races most of the time, but we're used to keeping busy and drowning it out.

The problem with a racing Monkey Mind

There are many physiological and psychological effects from a racing Monkey Mind. These include:

- **Stress hormones go wild.**

    Our fight / flight mechanism is regularly triggered by stressful thoughts and the sympathetic nervous system goes into overdrive. This can lead to fatigue, difficulty with concentration and, if it's regular, ill health.

- **Shallow breathing.**

    Shallow, upper-chest breathing is a common symptom of a racing mind. It reduces the amount of oxygen available to the body, which impacts everything from your cellular-level health to your mind's ability to think. Oxygen is the body's main food.

- **Foggy thinking.**

    With the reduced oxygen levels, your mind will struggle to think clearly. With the constant stream of Monkey Mind commentary, it's hard to access a state of mind that leads to insight and inspiration, so you're more likely to find it hard to complete even simple tasks, let alone complex jobs.

- **Stress creates stress.**

    A stressed-out mind is like a perpetual motion machine: it just keeps going. If your Monkey Mind is telling you stories of stress and worry, it will breed more stories to justify keeping that cycle going. It isn't going to stop, unless you do something differently.

Day 8

What's Going On When You Meditate?

What's still happening, when you're doing 'nothing' (also known as meditating!)?

Thinking! Thinking! Thinking!

Your Monkey Mind provides a constant stream of entertainment and distraction. It will be:

- Re-running events
- Giving a commentary on your current activity
- Analysing
- Understanding
- Passing judgement
- Worrying about the past or future
- Planning whatever is next
- Reminding you of stuff

It will be absolutely anywhere, other than 'here and now'.

Meditation invites us to sit with our thoughts; to stop fighting them; to stop resisting; to stop repressing them; to stop engaging with them - it's about becoming a silent, non-judgemental observer of our thoughts. As the psychotherapist Carl Jung famously said:

> *"What you resist persists."*
> *And that goes for your Monkey Mind, too.*

As soon as we resist a thought, we are giving it our power and attention. As soon as we fight it, it wins. We make it stronger by feeding it with our attention. Left to its own devices, it would simply melt away.

> *Many years ago a Buddhist monk taught me that no emotion or thought can last longer than 60 seconds without us 'feeding it' by telling ourselves stories or engaging with the thought.*
> *I found that really challenging at the time, because I was very good at being stuck in a particular emotion for days on end. But, with practice, I found what he said to be true.*

Day 8

> *A thought left to its own devices arrives,*
> *grows and then gently fades away.*
> *That is the natural course of the thought.*

The reason our thoughts hang around for so long is because we keep feeding them.

> *The more you try to stop your mind*
> *racing, the more it will resist your efforts.*
> *Acceptance of the mind is the key to inner*
> *peace.*

My invitation to you this week is:

Instead of fighting a thought, instead of trying to make your mind go quiet, how about becoming a conscious observer of your thoughts? And don't just leave it for your meditation practice time!

Allow yourself to become detached from your thoughts; stop telling the stories. Perhaps you might imagine your thoughts to be like soft clouds, floating across the sky - you observe them, but you are not engaging with them or trying to control them. And, just as mysteriously as they arrive, so they can leave.

Of if you prefer you might imagine the thought being on a conveyor belt, it arrives on the conveyor belt: you notice it and it moves away without you having to do anything. Remember the number one meditation myth? Meditation is NOT about shutting up your Monkey Mind – or getting rid of it! (See Day One).

But an untrained, untamed mind is like a sugar-laden, over-excited kid at Christmas. You can't expect it to behave calmly and it's likely to end in a tantrum.

So the goal of accepting your Monkey Mind is to stop resisting it, but also to stop engaging with it. Whereas the goal of your meditation practice is to teach it habits that lead to your inner peace, not to chaotic inner stress.

Day 8

> What you resist persists;
>
> and that goes for your monkey mind, too.
>
> CLARE JOSA
> (WITH A LITTLE HELP FROM CARL JUNG!)

Remember to breathe!

People sometimes find that they concentrate so hard on meditating that they hold their breath!

The idea is to be relaxed, but alert, in your meditative concentration and focus. So please remember to breathe - allow your breathing to be gentle and natural. If you need to, it can help to repeat the 3 sighing breaths from the beginning of the meditation, to help you to relax.

You can practise this any time of day - you don't need to wait for your meditation. In fact, if you practise relaxed belly breathing regularly, even just for 60 seconds, you will soon notice a dramatic reduction in your stress levels and a big improvement in the quality of your meditation experiences.

Day 8

Learning To Love Your Monkey Mind

Acceptance of our thoughts is one of the keys to meditation, to de-stressing, to feeling more calm and to feeling happier. Acceptance of our thoughts – instead of fighting them - is what we are going to be focusing on this week.

How about allowing your thoughts to turn into passing clouds, just for the next sixty seconds?

I hope you enjoy your new week two meditation. Remember, it's Track 2 of the MP3s (or optional CD) which accompany this book.

Namaste,

Clare

P. S. Tomorrow we'll be investigating how to stop others from stealing your meditation time.

P. P. S. Want to discover why making friends with your Monkey Mind could be the best move you ever make? There's a bonus article for you:

"How Falling In Love With Your Monkey Mind Can Be The Key To Inner Peace":

www.28DayMeditationChallenge.com/bonus

Day 8 Affirmation

I choose to start making friends with my Monkey Mind.

DAY 9

HOW TO STOP OTHERS FROM STEALING YOUR MEDITATION TIME

... And it's easier than you might think...

Day 9: How To Stop Others From Stealing Your Meditation Time

How did you get on with your first time listening to the week 2 meditation? Was it fun, watching your thoughts start to drift by? Did your mind play ball? Or did it come up with objections to the process? We'll be looking at how to handle your Monkey Mind's tricks over the coming days.

But today we're talking about how on earth you can stop others from stealing your meditation time.

This can be a real challenge, when starting a meditation journey.

I'm sure that some of you out there on the 28 Day Meditation Challenge have experienced this already, because you are trying to fit your new habit in as something extra, in a day that already feels pretty full. We start the day with the best of intentions, but suddenly it's bedtime and we're feeling too tired...

What steals our meditation time?

We all have our own personal favourites. It might be something unexpected that needs doing; it might be a phone call that overruns; it might be dealing with our messages; it might be something that comes up at work; it might be our family demands our attention. The list is as endless as our imagination.

What to do if it happens regularly?

If you notice that things are regularly interrupting your meditation space, then it really is time to take a look at your level of commitment to meditating... At risk of being shouted at, it is only ten minutes a day you are asking yourself for.

Is it really so difficult to find ten minutes for ourselves?

Day 9

Yes? Then perhaps you're running a bigger issue, which would benefit from being dealt with?

- Are you still waiting to be convinced of the benefits of your meditation practice?
- Perhaps you need to change habits about how you say yes to things?
- Perhaps it's something about not feeling that you deserve time for the things you want to do?
- Would you benefit from help from a wise friend on how to manage interruptions?
- It could be worth looking at what you're using the distractions to avoid?
- Are your meditation excuses getting in the way? (Day 3)

Treat It Like An Appointment

Of course it is important to be flexible in life. But just imagine how much easier it would be to fit your meditation in, if you treated it like an appointment - not negotiable.

For example you wouldn't cancel an optician's appointment, unless you really had to, would you?

So how about treating your meditation time the same way?

When you have that mind-set towards your meditating time, it's amazing how easy it is to brush away the interruptions that would otherwise have stopped you from you taking your ten minutes.

> *Taking your meditation time seriously is the key to finding the time to do it.*

Prioritising it over other things is essential, or you'll find yourself regularly missing it and not benefiting from it. While you list it as an 'optional' part of your day or a 'nice to have' activity, it is destined to fall off the bottom of your 'to do' list. **It is better to meditate for a shorter time, every day, than for a long time once in a blue moon.**

Day 9

Remember: when you are feeling calm and focused, when you have clarity and a smile on your face, the thing that was going to interrupt your meditation will be much easier to handle.

> Ten minutes for yourself.
> Give yourself this gift.
> Is it really so difficult?

Many of the people who have completed the 28 Day Meditation Challenge have found that they enjoy their meditation space so much - and it helps them so much - that sometimes they even do it twice a day!

There's no pressure for this, but if you can find the time, the benefits are amazing.

Day 9

Is it about needing to say "No"?

Maybe you could look at how you feel about saying no to people?

Or perhaps you could have a new phrase: *"Yes, when I have had my ten minutes to meditate"*? Most things will all wait for ten minutes, if we're really honest with ourselves.

What's the best time of day to meditate?

The key to success is to fit your meditation in at a time that works for you.

Traditionally, so we're told, we should meditate around 4am – there's not a chance of that for most of us! The next 'best' time is shortly after waking up. That's all very well if you live in an ashram - not so practical if you have a busy morning schedule when getting up earlier wouldn't work, especially if there are 'little people' in your life, who demand early morning attention.

Personally, the only space I get is in the evening, just after the children have fallen asleep – or incredibly early in the morning, before the rest of the family wakes up. And I've arranged things to work around that, because I know how different my day feels if I don't take that time to meditate.

What can you do?

Forget what people tell you about what time you should meditate! The best time for you to meditate is the time that works for you and for your day.

It might help you to set yourself a reminder. Resources like the Fungie bell (see below) or your computer's alarm / phone alarm can help remind you when your meditation time has arrived. Or you could use the reminder to practise five deep breaths, allowing your attention to rest on your breathing for a few moments.

Day 9

➡ For the link to the Fungie bell and other similar resources: www.28DayMeditationChallenge.com/bonus

Choosing a similar time each day, whenever that is, helps you to get into the routine.

Choosing the same place each day can help you get into the routine, too. Your mind and body quickly become anchored into the physical preparation for meditating, in a particular place, and this makes it easier to relax and feel calmer. It makes meditating less effort and more effective. (More on that later in the 28 days!).

Also, preparing in the same way sets off our unconscious mind's auto-pilot response, taking us back to a peaceful state of mind, fast.

You can prepare yourself by, for example:

- remembering to close the door
- lighting a candle
- sitting down
- putting a blanket around your shoulders

This physical preparation will trigger unconscious memories and automatically help you to relax, to feel more calm and to feel ready to meditate.

> ***Aside***: *there's a short, tongue-in-cheek video about the danger of listening to everything you're told about the traditions behind preparation for meditating, which you might find useful. You'll find the link with the other bonus materials on the website.*

Tell those that might need you during your meditation time that you are not around; you are not available, but you will be back soon! Take the phone off the hook; don't look at email messages just before you meditate, or they'll be preying on your mind.

This is your time and, believe me, those around you will eventually

Day 9

be grateful, because it will make a huge difference for you - and one day they will notice that difference, too.

> **Quick Exercise**
>
> I'm curious: what (or who!) typically steals your meditation time?
>
> And how do you handle it?
>
> How about sharing your answers with others?
>
> www.Facebook.com/28DayMeditationChallengeCourse

That's enough for now. I hope you enjoy your week two meditation today!

Namaste,

Clare

P. S. Tomorrow we're going to be looking at what your Monkey Mind is trying to tell you.

Day 9 Affirmation

My happiness is worth ten minutes a day of my time.

DAY 10

WHAT IS YOUR MONKEY MIND TRYING TO TELL YOU?

Discover how many games it likes to play while you're meditating.

Day 10

Day 10: What Is Your Monkey Mind Trying To Tell You?

I don't know about you, but most of us seem to have what the meditation world calls a Monkey Mind. I call it my grasshopper mind, because it can flit from one thing to the next with an amazing level of skill, constantly hopping around, making plenty of noise and rarely sitting still.

When we sit for silent meditation or try to practise mindfulness, we often find that our biggest challenges, such as knees hurting or back aching, are nothing compared to the chattering of our mind. Yet, although we might not be aware of where the thoughts come from, we can do something about them.

You don't have to ignore your Monkey Mind.

Remember the #1 meditation myth? **Meditation and mindfulness are *not* about making your Monkey Mind shut up!**

Sometimes our Monkey Mind is trying to get a message through to us.

It might be worried that we're going to forget to do something; sometimes it's telling us about things we are afraid of; sometimes it's just a habit. We are used to filling up the silence with chatter, so we don't feel lonely; sometimes we have just got into the habit of having an unconscious commentary running of everything we are seeing and doing.

When your Monkey Mind is shouting and yelling, it's worth sitting quietly for a moment and asking yourself why. Is there a message it's trying to get to you? Is there something you need to know?

Often, if you listen without judgement or interaction, the Monkey Mind can have its say and then relax. Sometimes it helps to jot down the thing it wanted you to remember, so you can let go of it and get on with your meditation.

Day 10

What Are Some Of The Games A Monkey Mind Can Play? And What Can You Do About Them?

I'm curious: what are the games that your Monkey Mind plays, when you're trying to meditate or practise mindfulness?

Here are some of the ways that previous students on the 28 Day Meditation Challenge have experienced it:

- **Getting bored**

    Your Monkey Mind tells you it's feeling bored. It tells you that meditation is boring. It can be pretty convincing.

    Of course meditation is boring for a Monkey Mind that is used to running the show, at faster than the speed of sound...

    But accepting that your mind is playing the 'bored game' and allowing yourself to go more deeply into your practice will prove to your Monkey Mind that meditation is far from boring!

- **Playing music**

    Our Monkey Mind has often been trained to be scared of silence. So, even if you manage to accept your thoughts, it might try new tactics, such as playing music or singing a catchy song.

    Again - just accept this. Stick the music on the conveyer belt or whichever other technique is working for you.

    Turn down the volume. Slow down the tempo, if it starts yelling for attention.

    Don't engage. Don't get annoyed. Don't play the game. Just practise accepting it and let it go. It will eventually get the idea.

- **Reminding you about your 'to do' list**

    Classic trick, this one! Again - you know it's not true. It's VERY rare that something won't wait ten minutes.

    Stick it on the conveyer belt!

Day 10

A previous 28 Day Meditation Challenge student shared:

> *"For the first time *ever* in lots of 'trying and failing', I got some sense of what it is like to watch thoughts and actually observe them, moving on. I love the conveyer belt."*

Another shared a great tip for accepting - and not engaging - with your thoughts:

> *"I chose to sit outside a cave, in the sunshine, while my thoughts stayed in the cave. They seemed quieter; more distant. And it made it harder for me to interact with them - easier to accept them and just let them be."*

Quick Exercise:

What are your Monkey Mind's games? They're different for each of us.

And how do you deal with them?

What has worked for you?

What could you do differently, to make peace with your Monkey Mind?

It's ok to get creative!

Do You See What's Going On?

Often we're not even aware of the fact that we're living our life according to the whim of the Monkey Mind. It is triggering our emotions and filtering our experience of life, without our conscious

Day 10

permission. Sounds scary? Yet this is what we have spent many years training it to do!

And we have spent a lifetime, learning to ignore its behaviour and pretend it isn't there.

The mind's 'default setting' is thinking, not awareness, peace, stillness or being. So it's no wonder that it objects, when we dare to suggest it might quieten down for our meditation time…

How To Tame A Multi-Tasking Mind

Many of us have trained our mind to need to think of many things at once. It's a real skill. But it doesn't help you to relax, de-stress or learn to meditate. An interesting question (that sends your mind into a spin!) is:

"What won't happen if I don't think of three things at once?"

Quick Exercise:

What won't happen if your mind doesn't chatter three conversations at once?

Just let an answer bubble up for you, without analysing or judging it.

This can help you unlock the key of why you have been feeding your Monkey Mind.

Are you scared of silence?

Are you scared things won't get done?

Are you trying to avoid thinking about something else?

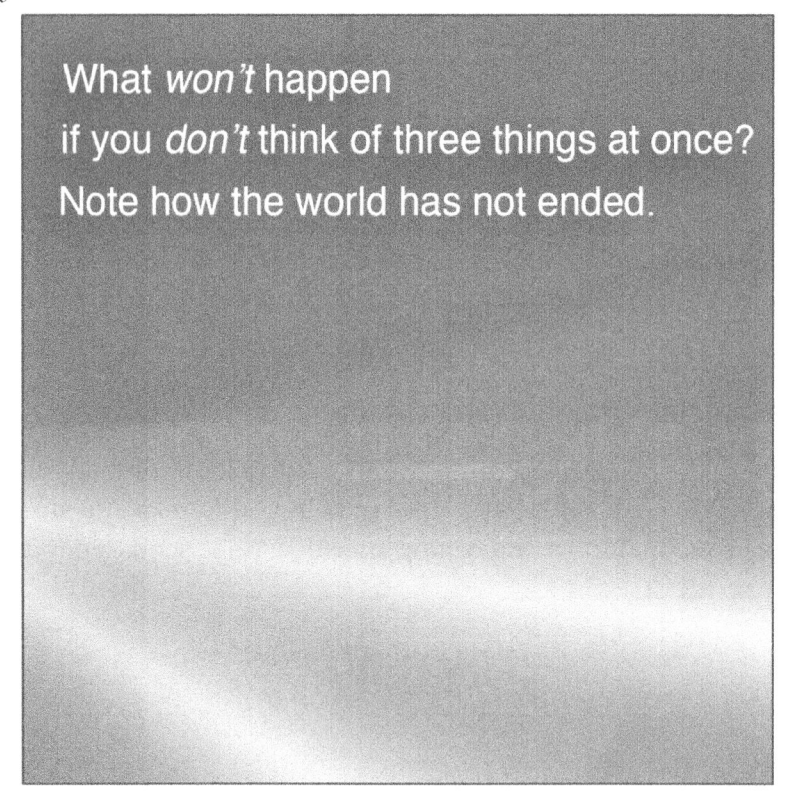

Day 10

> **What *won't* happen
> if you *don't* think of three things at once?
> Note how the world has not ended.**

Usually the answer to that question contains hints on how to set yourself free from that old grasshopper mind habit. If the answer feels uncomfortable, don't dive into the drama. Simply use it as an opportunity to practise acceptance.

Thinking isn't 'bad'. But an out-of-control mind produces thinking that is 'unconscious'; 'unaware'. This feeds our love of drama, creating painful emotional states and keeping us stuck worrying about the past or stressing about the future.

> *It is 'untamed' thinking that is the issue,
> not the presence of the thoughts.*

It is our attachment to the thoughts that causes the pain, not the fact that they exist.

Day 10

Be Gentle, But Firm, With Your Monkey Mind.

Having chosen to go on a meditation journey, you're already taking positive steps towards creating a new future.

Meditation and mindfulness can really, really help to calm a Monkey Mind, but you need to be careful which kind of meditation you pick. For example, the types of meditation where you sit silently for hours might not be the best place for you to start, if your Monkey Mind stresses you out.

> *Remember that with every breath we can choose to make a fresh start. Anything the Monkey Mind is telling us about our past belongs just there.*

Mindfulness, which we are looking at next week, is about being fully present and aware of the moment - including your thoughts. It can be a lot easier for somebody who's running a strong Monkey Mind pattern.

Practical solutions for today

You might like to experiment with some subtle tweaks you can make to remind your grasshopper mind who's in charge and calm it a little. You are the boss of your Monkey Mind, whether it accepts it or not!

If your thoughts are mainly words:

- How about telling your thoughts to slow down? Cutting the speed at which your mind is speaking can help to reduce your stress levels.
- And when you have played with that, how about changing the volume, making it quieter?
- You could experiment with changing the tone of the conversation that you are hearing in your head and making it sound kinder and softer.

Day 10

If your thoughts are mainly pictures:

- How about slowing down any movement in the pictures? This can really help you relax.
- If the pictures are bright and colourful, you could tone them down a little.
- If they are big, you could make them smaller.

All this - and plenty more - is possible. You just need to play with the techniques.

Don't wait till you're meditating - practise these techniques at any time of day when you want to quieten your mind and de-stress.

If your Monkey Mind is a bit rebellious, there's something you can do to get it to help you, instead of hindering your meditation journey:

Give your Monkey Mind a job to do, while you're meditating!

For example, it could be 'in charge' of reminding you to focus on your meditation, when your attention drifts. Or perhaps it might like to be the 'boss' of letting you know how your big toe on your left foot is feeling.

The job doesn't have to be serious!

Your mind is used to working very hard and, like any workaholic, it finds it hard to switch off. It deserves your compassion - but not your sympathy!

It's time for you to get back in the driving seat....

So my invitation to you today is to experiment with understanding what your Monkey Mind might be trying to tell you - and then to remind it who's boss - lovingly, but firmly.

Day 10

I really hope you enjoy today's meditation.

Namaste,

Clare

P. S. Tomorrow we'll be talking about how to stop your 'to do' list getting in the way!

> *Day 10 Affirmation*
>
> *I give my Monkey Mind permission to let go, just for ten minutes.*

DAY 11

HOW TO STOP YOUR 'TO DO' LIST GETTING IN THE WAY

Discover how regular meditation could even help make your 'to do' list shorter.

Day 11: How To Stop Your 'To Do' List Getting In The Way

A common objection I hear from students is that they've simply got too much to do, to be able to take ten minutes out to meditate or practise mindfulness.

We've all done it. We have all had the intention to meditate, but 'stuff got in the way'. Or, if we actually manage to meditate, suddenly our mind is full, reminding us of everything on our 'to do' list. When we sit still and stop being busy, we can instantly become aware of how much we still have to do and it can feel like our mind is racing even more than usual.

The key with this one is acceptance.

It's ok - just let your mind go on with the chattering, telling you about the vacuuming, telling you about the shopping, telling you about the school run... **Don't try to fight it or ignore it. It will eventually get the idea and calm down.**

And then you can start teaching it how to meditate with you, rather than being against you. You can learn how to use your mind to focus; how to use it to help you concentrate.

We all have plenty to do. The ironic thing is that when we are calm and relaxed we are able to get one thing finished at a time, and our 'to do' list gets done much more quickly. Also, the new-found clarity often helps us see things that didn't need to be on it in the first place.

Regular meditation helps us worry less, it helps us stress less, and it makes the 'to do' list easier.

Surely it's worth investing ten minutes of your time?

Day 11

The vacuuming can wait! Or, if you really find that the vacuuming has to be done, by all means to do it, but commit to meditating immediately afterwards – and perhaps do the vacuuming mindfully?!

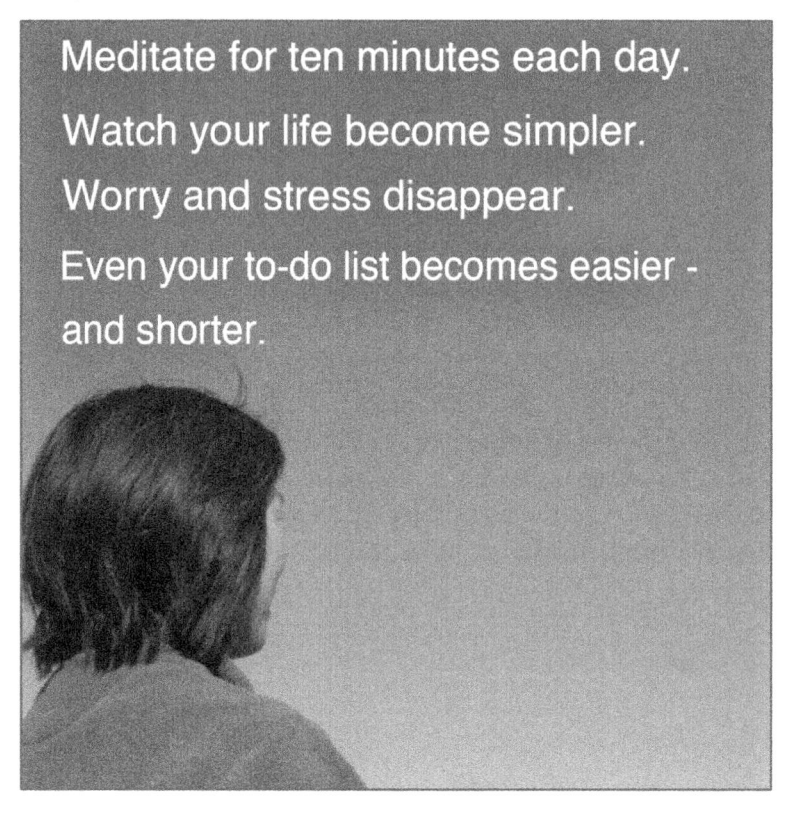

> Meditate for ten minutes each day.
> Watch your life become simpler.
> Worry and stress disappear.
> Even your to-do list becomes easier - and shorter.

When you hit your 80th birthday party, I am pretty sure you're going to look back and feel grateful for the number of times you've meditated - those meditation times that have given you inner peace and happiness - rather than the number of times you vacuumed your house or checked your emails

It's very likely that you'll feel happiest about the times you told yourself, "I choose...", rather than those when you said, "I should..."

Day 11

There's no need to feel guilty

Choosing to meditate - temporarily postponing your 'to do' list - gives you more energy and clarity of thinking. The increased focus and concentration helps you to get more done, more quickly, as well as prioritising and dumping the stuff that isn't really essential. How about throwing away that guilt right now? Feeling guilty has no place in your meditation practice. You either choose to meditate, or you don't. It's your choice. And it's only for ten minutes. If the phone rang right now, I bet you'd find ten minutes to talk to someone, wouldn't you?

So the next time your 'to do' list gets in the way, thank your mind for reminding you about what needs to be done and then how about telling it, "The next ten minutes are mine"?

My personal time management secret

The most useful resource I have ever found to help me break the habits that were stealing all my spare time is the **4 Hour Work Week by Tim Ferriss**.

Whether or not you want to reduce your working hours, many of his suggestions throw conventional time management (which is all about 'doing, doing, doing') on its head.

His proven strategies apply to all of us and they might just change your life. They'll certainly help you find ten minutes a day to meditate. Without them, I would never have found time, with 3 young boys, to create this course for you!

Find out more about Tim Ferriss's suggestions and how they could work for you:
www.28DayMeditationChallenge.com/bonus

Day 11

I hope you enjoy today's meditation.

Namaste,

Clare

P. S. If you'd like some extra inspiration to help you with this week's meditation, there's a bonus article here:

"How Falling In Love With Your Monkey Mind Can Be The Key To Inner Peace"

www.28DayMeditationChallenge.com/bonus

P. P. S. Tomorrow I'll be sharing some insider secrets on how to turn your new meditation practice into a long-term habit.

Day 11 Affirmation

I allow my meditation time to become a priority.

DAY 12

HOW TO CREATE A MEDITATION HABIT

Discover the insider secrets to fast track creating any new habit.

Day 12

Day 12: Insider Secrets: How To Create The Meditating Habit

The easiest way to create habit is to choose to do it.

I know that probably sounds stupid, but it's amazing how often we try and create a habit, **when we haven't really bought into the change we want to make**. We are doing it because somebody else tells us to or we think we ought to.

The easiest way to create a habit is to really understand why you want to do it (that's why we covered it back in the 'Getting Started' section on page 36). Then all you need to do is create a rhythm in your day; a routine; something that will remind you to do it and something that will help you celebrate the fact that you did. It also helps if you keep track of the progress you are making.

The 3 steps to a new habit:

- Inspiration is what gives us the idea to get started.
- Motivation really gets us going.
- But it is routine and consistent efforts that, together, create the change.

Ancient Sanskrit (the language in which many of the ancient meditation practices were originally taught) has a special word for this consistent effort: **abhyasa**. Without abhyasa, even the most enthusiastic student is unlikely to see tangible progress. So motivating yourself to make your meditation time an integral part of your daily routine is crucial for achieving the results you are looking for – and learning to meditate.

> *I like to think of abhyasa as doing what I know needs to be done, even when I don't feel like it. And I always feel better afterwards.*

Day 12

*Abhyasa – dedication; commitment; despite distractions.
You won't make progress on your meditation journey without it.*

Quick Exercise:

Think of an example in the past where you have motivated yourself to do something – and to keep going with it.

How did you motivate yourself?

What worked for you?

What didn't work?

How did you remind yourself to keep going?

What kinds of incentives worked?

How did you create and then establish the change in your routine?

How could you apply that to help yourself with your meditation practice?

How about sharing your answers?

www.Facebook.com/28DayMeditationChallengeCourse

Apply what you know works for you and then, over time, as your skill improves, you'll find you really enjoy your ten minutes of meditation. You'll find yourself looking forward to it. You'll crave it, as your personal space and quiet time. And if you miss it, you'll feel it throughout your day. When you get to that stage, the meditation is then driving itself.

Day 12

> *Once you have created the rhythm – the routine – the change becomes a habit.*

An easy way to create the meditation routine is to do it at the same time, in the same place, each day. Then your body and mind come to expect it. And if you need to set yourself a reminder - be it an alarm or a piece of paper on the fridge door - do it! It's ok.

> *Creating a new habit is as much about remembering to do it as it is about the new techniques.*

Once you see positive results, your new habit will become self-sustaining. While you are getting to that point, the routine and the habit are the key.

Picking the same point in your daily routine to meditate gets you anchored into the rhythm. If excuses and interruptions are getting in the way, deal with them! You can - you know you can. Nothing is impossible!

> *For example, if you had a habit of buying a doughnut every time you walk past the baker at 11 o'clock in the morning, your body and mind would become conditioned to expect it. Your body and mind will even give you signals, to remind you to go past the baker, should you forget to on a particular day.*

It Is The Same With Meditation.

If, at the same point in time in our routine each day, we go to the same place, sit in the same way and say to ourselves, "This is my meditation time," it doesn't take long before your body and your mind start remembering what comes next. They'll remember that it feels good and they'll start nudging you to meditate.

Feeling irritated is often the signal that it's time to meditate - so be aware of this! You'll notice if you have a day when, maybe, your

Day 12

meditation time has to move, your body will start to get ready for it at the time you usually meditate.

Millennia of meditation students have discovered that knowing how to meditate isn't enough - you need to know how to create the habit..

It's knowing how to create the habit that makes the difference between a 'nice idea' and a strong, sustainable meditation or mindfulness practice.

That's the key aim of the 28 Day Meditation Challenge.

> The easiest way to create a new habit is simply to choose to do it.

So the rhythm, the routine and the habit are what create a long-term meditation practice - and that is what will get you the results you are looking for.

Day 12

In the world of psychology and NLP, this is known as anchoring. It's an incredibly useful technique.

If you'd like to find out more about it, here's a bonus article:

"How To Use Anchoring To Help You Remember To Meditate."

www.28DayMeditationChallenge.com/bonus

I really hope you enjoy your meditation today.

Namaste,

Clare

P. S. Tomorrow we'll be looking at how to handle feeling too tired to meditate!

Day 12 Affirmation

I choose to take actions that support my meditation habit.

DAY 13

ARE YOU TOO TIRED TO MEDITATE?

Find out why meditation might be the last thing you need.

Day 13

Day 13: Are You Too Tired To Meditate?

Do you ever find you're too tired or stressed to meditate?

> *Back in the days when I was training to become a meditation teacher, I was on the course with my husband Peter. He was famous for his 'nodding dog' impressions. You would get 15 to 20 minutes into a meditation technique and suddenly there would be a nearly-silent giggle from the tutor at the front of the room, as they saw him nodding away, falling asleep. As usual, he was too tired to meditate.*

Now that might seem strange, because we might wonder, "It's meditation: I am sitting still; I'm relaxing; I've got my eyes closed, how can I stay awake?". . . But actually meditation is about relaxed alertness. That's the difference between deep relaxation - which is intending solely to relax you - and meditation, which is about relaxation with focus and concentration.

And it reminded me of my meditation mentor, Chris Barrington (www.DruWorldwide.com), and a story he once told.

> *A severely stressed executive came to him, wanting to learn to meditate. It didn't take long to see that the guy couldn't sit still: fingers twitching, body fidgeting, fast upper-chest breathing, super-fast talking... You could see his mind was racing and the bags under his eyes told tales of stress-filled sleepless nights. And, once he got to meditate, he would pretty much instantly fall asleep. If anyone ever needed to tap into the de-stressing benefits of deep relaxation, this guy was a prime candidate.*
> *But my mentor turned him away.*
> *"Why on earth would you do that?" we asked him; a stunned class of trainee teachers. He smiled gently as he explained that to be able to meditate there are three stages you have to go through.*

*Meditation is about relaxation, acceptance and **then** focused concentration.*

Day 13

Until you can relax, you can't meditate.

If you find it really hard to sit still, if you're finding it really hard to accept your mind, if you're finding it impossible to manage those pesky thoughts, it could be that what you need most right now is actually deep relaxation and not meditation. It takes a lot of energy to manage and accept your thoughts. It takes energy to concentrate and focus. That's why we make more mistakes, for example, when writing a message if we're tired, than if we're feeling refreshed. So feeling too tired to be able to meditate effectively is a common problem.

Fortunately, there's a simple solution: no, it's not sleep! It's deep relaxation.

> *Doing a 20 minute progressive tense and release deep relaxation every evening, even just for a week, can transform your experience of life.*

I'm not exaggerating!

It can have the most profound effect on your body's production of adrenalin and other stress hormones, allowing you to relax and recharge your batteries.

Once you are able to relax, then you will find meditation MUCH easier. It might be that you need to go and spend a month doing that, before you come back and maybe re-start the 28 Day Meditation Challenge (I'm not trying to get rid of you!). Or, if you are prepared to carve out the time you could do both at once.

Deep relaxation is absolutely key to our health, especially when we are running on adrenalin. This constant, low-level stress means that – for many of us - our adrenal glands are nearly empty and our mind and body are close to burn-out. We survive on a diet of stimulants – usually caffeine, sugary foods and high carbohydrate foods, to give us the 'boost' we need to keep going. But we're paying a big price.

Day 13

> **Aside**: *if this is resonating for you, you might want to check out the best book I have ever found on dealing with long-term exhaustion and adrenal issues. It's called* **'Adrenal Fatigue'** *by* **James Wilson** *and reading it changed my life – despite the fact I thought that, as a Meditation Teacher and NLP Trainer, I already knew all there was to know about dealing with stress...*

To find out more about his ground-breaking work, check out the resources at:

www.28DayMeditationChallenge.com/bonus

The other thing that can make a huge difference to being able to relax is your posture - as we mentioned on Day 2. If your back posture is activating your sympathetic nervous system (fight / flight) without also triggering your parasympathetic relaxation response, you could end up too tense and 'fired-up' to be able to meditate effectively.

Watch out for your emotions

Often, when starting a new meditation or mindfulness habit, we have been feeling tired for a very long time. Our Monkey Mind drowns out the tiredness with its constant commentary.

When we learn how to stop and rest, the old tiredness and even long-suppressed emotions can come out to play. If you're feeling very tired, do a deep relaxation. If you're feeling emotional, there are some great techniques later in the 28 Day Meditation Challenge.

So what happened to the super-stressed executive?

> *He spent a few months working on deep relaxation and dealing with his stress habits. When he came back, ready to meditate, he got fast results. His body was able to relax easily, which made it much easier to accept his environment, his thoughts and his physical world. He was finally able to concentrate and meditate.*

Day 13

And, as for Peter?

> *You can always tell when he's too tired to meditate, because his now-infamous nodding dog returns. It's his personal tip-off that he's been over-doing things and needs to shift down a gear for a while.*

> Relax.
> Only then can you begin to meditate.

So my invitation to you today is to think about how you are living, how your body feels, how your mind feels and to see whether deep relaxation and de-stressing might be what you're secretly craving right now.

Want To Do A Guided Deep Relaxation Today?

There are plenty of good deep relaxation CDs / MP3s out there.

Day 13

However, as a bonus, to save you going shopping for another recording, I have included a 23 minute deep relaxation on Track 5 of the MP3s (or optional CD) which accompany this book.

I hope you enjoy it!

You can download your MP3 version here:

www.28DayMeditationChallenge.com/bonus

Namaste,

Clare

P. S. Tomorrow is your half-way point - we're going to be talking about how to handle it if you don't get instant results.

Day 13 Affirmation

I choose to look after my energy levels.

DAY 14

BUT I'VE NOT HAD INSTANT RESULTS!

How to keep yourself motivated, even if progress feels slow.

Day 14

Day 14: But I've Not Had Instant Results!

Congratulations! You're at the 2 week point - half way through your 28 day challenge.

How's it feeling? What have you learned so far? Are you finding it easier to make the space and time for your meditation? How did you find this week's meditation, compared to last week's?

Today we're talking about how to keep motivated until you see the results from your meditation.

Remember how you used to give yourself time to learn?

When we were learning to read as children, we knew that it would take time, concentration and focus. Learning the new skill was about learning from what worked and what didn't – making mistakes – and then creating the habit. Whether it was crawling, walking, eating with a fork or learning to read, we used to give ourselves time to get things sussed.

Yet with things like meditation, it's amazing how often we expect to achieve results akin to enlightenment in the space of the first few days. It's easy to fall into the trap of expecting to tame decades' worth of an unruly mind in just a few short weeks. Ok, maybe I'm exaggerating a bit, but we beat ourselves up pretty quickly when we don't achieve near-instant results.

> *Anyone who learns to play a musical instrument knows that the early stages can be tricky, as you learn so much about how to handle the instrument: how to control the sounds it makes, how to relax into playing it.*
> *It is said that it takes 10,000 hours of practice to become a virtuoso. But you don't have to go that far to enjoy playing music. There are plenty of stopping points along the way.*
> *And it's the same with meditation. You don't have to be an expert meditator, to enjoy it and reap the benefits.*

Day 14

I often hear people lamenting at about this stage that their mind is still chattering away and that they find it hard to maintain ten minutes' focus. That's ok! You're human! Meditation is a skill that needs practice. And remember the #1 meditation myth from Day 1?

> **Quick Exercise:**
>
> So my questions for you this morning are (allow yourself time to think about this one):
>
> What have you been expecting from your meditation practice?
>
> What are you hoping will happen for you?
>
> And, being honest, how soon were you expecting to experience that?

The dangers of expectations

When we place an expectation on our meditation, it becomes a box that confines our experience of the process.

We unconsciously look for things that support that expectation. If our expectation falls within the box, then great. If it's not as good, we feel like a failure. Those of us running perfectionism traits will tend to beat ourselves up over it, big time. It's like a limiting belief causing us to sabotage what we are trying to achieve.

It takes time and dedication to be able to meditate. It's like any other skill, in that respect. And the best thing we can do to support our learning is to approach each meditation with an open mind and without attachment to previous experiences or expectations of the next one.

Day 14

> *Meditation can be a profoundly powerful and beautiful experience, but we have to practice it to get results.*

Our meditations might be very different every day.

Some days you might really feel you've reached a place of inner peace and calm. And that can set up a whole new level of expectation… On other days you might wonder, "Why did I bother doing that?". It is all part of the meditation journey, it is all part of the learning process. Here are some suggestions to help you notice the improvements and progress you are making.

- **How about keeping a mood diary?**
  At the end of each day, how about jotting down a few notes of the kinds of emotions you were feeling? In just a few weeks, you will notice how you are able to ride the waves of life and your emotions more easily. When you see this, congratulate yourself. Meditation goes much deeper than the ten minutes a day you're spending on it; it impacts all areas of your life, so if you're not seeing the results you had hoped for, bear in mind that you might be looking for progress in the wrong place!

- **Trust the process**
  How many millions of people across the world have found meditation helpful, over the millennia? Why should you be any different? If you keep practising you are going to get there.

- **Be realistic**
  Blissful enlightenment may well be possible on your first sitting, but it is unusual… One session is unlikely to take away all of your stresses and cares. Let the process work. Give it time to take root and grow.

> *Beating yourself up over not developing a new skill fast enough is a learned habit.*

Day 14

Think about it: when we were learning to walk or talk or eat - things we now take for granted - we made mistakes. It went wrong. We spilled food down our front, we fell over, we got our sentences muddled up. We didn't beat ourselves up - we picked ourselves up and we kept going, because we knew the process of gentle, determined practice would work.

> **Beating yourself up hasn't exactly worked over the years.**
> **How about encouraging yourself instead?**
> **How about starting today?**

Beating ourselves up about not picking up a skill instantly is a habit we acquire, rather than a natural state of 'humanness'. So the great news is that you can choose to unlearn that habit!

You can choose to stop beating yourself up. After all:

Beating yourself up hasn't exactly been working over the years, so how about encouraging yourself, instead?

Day 14

How about starting today?

How about starting to think about your meditation journey as a process, which you know is going to work?

Your job is simply to create the habit and then to allow yourself to enjoy the journey. And that's exactly what the 28 Day Meditation Challenge is all about.

Wishing you a very lovely Day 14!

Namaste,

Clare

P. S. Tomorrow we'll be moving on to discover the secrets of mindfulness.

Day 14 Affirmation

In this moment, I choose to encourage myself and celebrate the progress I have made.

Week Three

Welcome to week three!

This week includes one of my personal favourites, when it comes to meditation – bringing that sense of peace and awareness into everyday actions – mindful living.

It is the key to so many of the techniques in the world of meditation, as well as offering you the opportunity to transform your experience of life, whilst doing simple actions like drinking a cup of tea.

It really is like a magic trick.

This week I'll be sharing practical mindfulness techniques with you, helping you see how you've already been practising mindfulness, giving you a magic wand to deal with worrying, spilling the beans on how wiggling your butt can help you meditate and sharing secrets for what to do if meditation stirs that old emotional pot.

Enjoy!

Namaste,

Clare. ♡

DAY 15

WHAT ON EARTH IS MINDFULNESS?

Discovering the magic of living in the 'here and now'.

Day 15: What On Earth Is Mindfulness?

Welcome to week 3!

Are you ready to move on to the next phase of your meditation journey? Would you like to discover what mindfulness is? Want to find out why it's so important? Are you ready to bring it into your life - every day - easily helping you to feel calmer, happier and less stressed?

Being mindful is a state of being - a particular way of choosing to experience life, in the present moment.

Normally we let our mind run riot over past mistakes and get its knickers in a twist over future worries, whilst half sleep-walking our way through what is actually going on around us.

We're normally too busy being 'mind-full' to be 'mindful'.

Are you too 'mind-full'?

Here are some common symptoms of 'mindlessness' or being 'mind-full'.

- Do you find yourself 'listening' to someone, whilst thinking about your response?
- Do you realise you didn't really hear what they were saying?
- Do you find yourself getting to the bottom of a cup of tea or coffee, without remembering drinking it?
- Do you forget where you put things?
- Do you walk into a room, but can't remember why?
- Do you find yourself arriving at a destination, but not remembering the route you took?
- Do you find it hard to remember people's names?

Day 15

All of these - and plenty more - are symptoms of a mind so full of yesterday, tomorrow and 'what ifs', that it can't enjoy the present moment.

What's the problem with 'mindlessness'?

> *The 'present moment' - 'here and now':*
> *it's the only time you have.*

Yesterday is done and dusted. Tomorrow isn't here yet. If you want to actually live your life, then now is the only time you can do it. Want to make changes in the future? Then you need to do them now. Want to create a past that you're proud of? Then you need to take action now.

But that's tough, when we don't even notice eating our breakfast or driving to work!

Being mindful means dragging ourselves back into the present moment - away from the 'to do' list, the housework, next week's big meeting, last week's presentation and everything else that normally fills our mind to bursting point.

> *Are you too busy pretending you're a*
> *'human doing' to be a 'human being'?*

We might feel scared that, by being in the present moment, the 'to do' list will get forgotten; the shopping won't get done; the kids won't get fed. (Don't worry - they'll remind you!) But, in fact, it's the other way round.

By focussing our experience right here, right now, we can develop a clarity that somehow creates more time in our day, meaning the 'to do' list gets shorter and becomes less of an obsession.

> *When you are totally aware of what you*
> *are doing – 'doing with awareness' – it's*
> *amazing how much more easily life flows.*

Day 15

By getting back into the 'now', we can start to reconnect with the part of us that makes the unconscious choices about how to think, feel and act, in every single moment.

We start to experience the truth of life, rather than the story, stress and drama.

We get our thoughts, feelings and actions back under conscious control, breaking long-held habits of automatic responses to what psychologists call 'stimuli', but the rest of us call 'difficult people' or 'stressful situations'.

What exactly is mindfulness?

I'm going to give you a practical definition of what mindfulness is, rather than a spiritual or religious definition:

Day 15

Mindfulness is about actually experiencing life, while you're living it.

We tend to spend most of our time running away from our experience of life – hiding from it – because the stories our Monkey Mind tells us create pain. Mindfulness is about being present to your experience of life, as it truly is, rather than wanting to change it or believing the drama and the stories.

As Thich Nhat Hanh, a Zen Buddhist Master, tells us:

> *"To be mindful means to be here, fully present, and fully alive, unencumbered by thoughts of the past or the future, our worries or our projects. It is only when we stop that we can encounter life."*

As a meditation technique, mindfulness is about using your focus and concentration to be aware of the present moment, rather than being lost in the future or worrying about the past. However it's not about pretending that there wasn't a future or a past. It's about drawing your awareness back into your physical body and experiencing life through all of your senses; being truly present.

It is the kind of experience you get when you look into somebody's eyes and you really connect. You know that they're there and so are you. Rather than talking to them whilst maybe thinking about your shopping list and what you have got to cook for dinner, you're really 'present' with them.

Mindfulness is about living life as the sensory experience that it really is, in our physical bodies, rather than being stuck in our thinking mind. It's ideal for a multi-tasking mind, because it gives your mind something to do! It gets to help run the process of 'being here'.

Just imagine…

- actually tasting your tea, as you drink it
- really feeling that cuddle
- really hearing the birdsong

Day 15

- really smelling your coffee
- really seeing the beauty of the sun, peeping through the clouds
- really hearing what a loved-one is saying - and seeing the look in their face, when they know they have been heard
- actually feeling the comfort of your clothes on your body
- feeling your feet connect with the earth, with every step

Why settle for half-living?

The back of my business cards has a provocative quote, that sometimes gets me into trouble... It is:

Just because you're breathing, it doesn't mean you're alive.

But it sums up beautifully the difference between a life that is lived from the position of the Monkey Mind and a life that is lived with awareness – mindfully.

Mindfulness can bring your experience of life alive.

It is something you can do at any time, in any place, it feels great - and it's free - wow!

Mindfulness doesn't take up your time

One of the great bonuses of mindfulness is that, as you become more familiar with how to practise it, it doesn't take up any extra time. You can do it wherever and whenever you want to, no matter how busy you are. Plus it can help you de-stress, calm down, feel more relaxed, consciously choose your experience of life and set yourself free from living on auto-pilot.

The power of mindfulness to change the way we think, feel and behave is so strong that even traditional medical doctors are now

Day 15

using mindfulness to help people who are suffering from clinical depression. Universities are researching it. Mindfulness is also used in the training for all sorts of sports, where athletes really need moment-to-moment concentration and focus.

Imagine living your day actually being 'here' rather than, as I often call it, off on another planet or off with the fairies!

> *Mindfulness is an amazing de-stressing, relaxation technique, which comes with the added bonus that it makes life come to life.*

Want to give it a go?

This week's meditation guides you through silent sitting, which is one way of experiencing mindfulness.

You'll find the week 3 meditation is Track 3 of the MP3s (or optional CD) which accompany this book. As usual, the transcript is in Appendix A.

The messages this week will help you discover and experiment with techniques that you can weave into your daily life, if you so choose.

As with all of these techniques, the key is consistent, but relaxed, practice – remember the abhyasa (Day 12)? Play with these techniques, rather than forcing them. Notice your mind's objections (mindfulness helps to calm a chattering mind), but don't engage with the story.

In week one, we practised becoming grounded and simple breathing awareness - both of which are actually mindfulness techniques. In week two, we practised 'thought awareness' and playing gently with letting our thoughts pass through our minds, rather than clinging to them. This is another mindfulness technique. These two weeks have been important preparation for increasing your awareness of your physical, emotional and mind states, to help you get ready for impacting them, consciously, through mindful practices. The relaxation and stillness you have been cultivating are essential foundations to make mindfulness easier for you.

This week you will still be doing a (new) ten minute silent sitting meditation, and you'll also get the opportunity to bring your meditation - your mindfulness - into all your activities, if you want to. Even tasks like walking across the car park at work or doing the laundry can become a playground for practising being mindful. The more you play with it, the more you will feel radiantly alive.

I can't promise to make you a mindfulness expert in the next seven days, but it is my deepest wish that you feel inspired by some of what we cover and start a journey of mindfulness practice that could change your life.

When you have experienced this week's meditation, how about checking out this bonus article on the bell it uses.

"How Can A Sound Feel So Real?"

www.28DayMeditationChallenge.com/bonus

Namaste,

Clare

P. S. Tomorrow I'll be sharing one of my favourite 'do it anywhere' mindfulness techniques.

Day 15 Affirmation

In this moment, I choose to feel truly alive.

DAY 16

IS IT TIME TO TASTE YOUR TEA?

My favourite 'do it anywhere' mindfulness technique.

Day 16: Is It Time To Taste Your Tea?

Do you ever get to the end of a cup of tea (or whatever else you're drinking) with no recollection of drinking it?

Or do you find yourself drinking your tea, whilst thinking about everything else you have to do?

Does that actually get any of it done?

Thought not...!

Today I am inviting you to taste your tea.

It's a classic exercise that you can do to practice mindfulness. And the brilliant thing is that it doesn't take up much time, yet it brings huge benefits.

Day 16

The next time you make yourself a drink (hot, cold, it doesn't matter), I invite you to:

1. **Sit down with it.**
   Don't drink it on the run.

2. **Before you pick it up and drink it, actually look at it.**
   Really drag all of your awareness into the process of seeing what you see.

   Notice the glass, cup or mug it's in.

   Really see how the light reflects off it.

   Allow yourself to see the textures. There might be steam of ice-cold bubbles. Notice what you notice, in minute detail.

3. **Pick it up and notice the tactile feel of the cup or glass.**
   How does it feel in your hands? Perhaps there is a warmth or a coolness?

   Is it smooth? How heavy is it?

   Really allow your full awareness to rest in your fingertips for a few moments as you hold the drink.

4. **Before you drink the drink, take a sniff and allow yourself to become aware of the aroma.**
   Spend a moment allowing the smell to fill your awareness, letting your concentration gently rest on your drink.

5. **As you start to drink, sipping gently or gulping, it's up to you, allow yourself to really taste your drink.**
   Taste your tea, taste your water, whatever it is you're drinking. Experience the sensation over your tongue and your taste buds.

6. **And, as you swallow, allow yourself to hear the sounds.**
   Hear your swallowing. Perhaps there are other sounds, too?

Be completely aware of and fully present to the experience of 'tasting your tea'.

Day 16

> **Quick Exercise:**
>
> At the end of this process, take a moment to reflect. What did you notice?
>
> How do you feel now?
>
> How could you play with this mindfulness exercise, during your day?
>
> Want to share your answers?
>
> www.Facebook.com/28DayMeditationChallengeCourse

Once you are used to this, it takes no time at all. Your cup of tea (or whatever) becomes an unconscious anchor to help you remember to be mindful - to come back to the 'now' - to experience life, rather than your Monkey Mind's story of life.

Even if you are talking to someone or working on your computer as you drink your tea, every time you pick up your mug for another sip you can return to that calm place of being mindful, even if just for a few moments.

Many people find this technique is an amazing way to de-stress, to feel calmer and to feel more grounded and centred.

Normally we would make a cup of tea in a hurry, get to the end of the cup and then wonder where it went. We drink unconsciously, we eat unconsciously, we live unconsciously, as though we are half-asleep.

> *Practising this mindful interaction with everyday experiences is the fastest way to learn mindfulness – and change your life.*

It's a fast track on your meditation journey, because you are constantly bringing yourself back into the physical body and allowing yourself to focus and concentrate, in a relaxed way. Tasting

Day 16

your tea doesn't actually take any longer than drinking a cup of tea normally would. Yet it has so many benefits for you!

One of the knock-on effects of this kind of practice is that you won't lose your keys again. When we do things mindfully, we remember where we put the keys; we don't leave jobs half done; it's easier to concentrate; we stop running on adrenalin. Life becomes so much easier, more flowing, less stressful.

Mindful awareness - being present in the moment and actually experiencing life- is an amazingly simple technique to transform how you experience your life. Regular practice will reduce your stress levels, helping you to feel calmer and happier.

Of course, tasting your tea is just an example. This technique can be applied to any area of your life. 'Tasting your tea' can be used as a reminder to choose to return to the present moment and to truly experience life.

Who'd have thought that the simple act of tasting your tea could change your life?

Namaste,

Clare

P. S. Tomorrow you get the chance to discover a magic wand, to help you give up worrying, for good!

Day 16 Affirmation

Today, in this moment, I choose to 'taste my tea'.

DAY 17

WANT A MAGIC WAND FOR WORRYING?

How the secret of mindfulness can help you stop worrying & feel happier.

Day 17

Day 17: Want A Magic Wand For Worrying?

> *"Life isn't as serious as the mind makes it out to be." Eckhart Tolle*

Many of us are what could be called 'natural born worriers'.

It's an epidemic, which we do our best to make contagious. Yet it never, ever brings happiness or inner peace - and it rarely even creates the future we are hoping for. Esther Hicks has a lovely way of looking at it:

> *"Worrying is a way of creating a future you don't really want." Esther Hicks*

It is a fact of life that we tend to get the things that we give our attention to.

> *I remember, many years ago, when I was learning to drive, that I would steer towards whatever I was looking at. If I got distracted by somebody on the pavement, I would unconsciously steer the wheel in the direction of my focus. If I looked over at my driving instructor, he knew that he was going to have to grab the steering wheel - fast.*

Life is just the same. We tend to move towards that which has our focus and attention. But most of the time we're running on auto-pilot, so we don't even notice where that focus and attention is. We are at risk of worrying our way into a future we don't really want, without even noticing!

Meditation and mindfulness really help, by bringing us back to the present moment.

The techniques help us to relax, helping us to focus and concentrate. Then we can have clarity to see the difference between what is 'real' and what is the projection of our mind's story.

Meditation and mindfulness help us to break free of the story that

Day 17

we normally tell ourselves, the one that goes round and round in our heads, causing so much frustration and pain. The 'story' is what keeps us stuck, heading in a direction we didn't want to go in. The story might be a retelling of past hurts and failures, a constant reminder of our excuses and limiting beliefs or perhaps a running commentary and critique of our observations of life.

Yes, thinking is important. But most of our thinking is a waste of time.

By allowing ourselves to access a point of inner stillness and inner calm, which is what meditation helps us do, whenever we are feeling worried we know we can go back there and let go of those worries. When we have done that, for even just ten minutes, the worries don't seem so real any more.

Which seeds are you watering?

Our mind could be considered to be full of seeds - seeds of happiness, seeds of anger, seeds of excitement, seeds of worry – all waiting to grow. Our experience of life depends on which seeds we are watering. Watering our 'worrying seeds' (the general worrying about "What if this happens? What if that happens?") does nothing other than make us feel miserable and stressed! And it will make it more likely that we'll create circumstances that will allow those things to happen.

Meditation and mindfulness can help to calm a worrying mind, setting you free to choose which seeds to water; helping you to feel happier. Then you can create the space to ask yourself that magic question, *"What do I want instead?"*

Then you take action.

It can dramatically impact your experience of life, if you are ready to trust yourself and let go of worrying. It helps by allowing you to spot the gap between the stimulus and your auto-pilot response, so you can regain your choice - you can choose whether or not to feel

Day 17

worried or stressed. It puts you back in the driving seat, reclaiming your personal power.

Mindfulness and meditation help us to learn how to stop and become non-judgemental observers of our thoughts – even the negative ones – without getting caught up in them.

If you'd like to discover more about this, I've written an article for you about it:

"How Mindfulness Can Give You Back Your Choice"

www.28DayMeditationChallenge.com/bonus

> Life isn't as serious as the mind makes it out to be.
> ECKHART TOLLE

Want to know how you can quickly and easily use mindfulness techniques to help reduce worrying?

Day 17

Here's a sixty second technique that can turn things around – and no one will notice you're doing it!

Mindful Breathing – A Magic Wand
- Stop whatever you are doing and take a deep breath in to your belly. Breathe out with an 'ahhhh' sound, as you relax your body and mind. Do this 3 times. (You can do this silently and imagine saying 'ahhhh', if you're not alone).
- Now allow your breathing to settle into a natural rhythm.
- Bring all of your focus to your breathing.
- As you breathe in, you might like to mentally say something like, "I breathe in."
- As you breathe out, you might like to mentally say something like, "I breathe out."
- If you are feeling particularly stressed, you might choose phrases such as "I breathe in relaxation; I breathe out stress and worry."
- Repeat this for ten breaths. Do it in a relaxed way, with a gentle smile on your face.
- When you feel you have 'tuned in' to your breathing, you might like to briefly think back to whatever was worrying you and ask yourself, "What is real in this?" It helps you to detach from the story and the worry and helps to steer your mind back in the direction of solutions, rather than problems.
- Then ask yourself the 'magic questions':
    - *"Is this really what I want?"*
    - and, if it isn't, then *"What do I want instead?"*

This technique is a wonderfully fast de-stressing tool, as well as being useful mindfulness practice. **If you can take one peaceful breath, you can take another... and another.**

Paying attention to your breathing helps your body to relax and your mind to return to the present moment.

Day 17

> *Breath awareness is a core mindfulness technique.*

You focus on one breath at a time. The last breath has gone. Your next breath hasn't yet arrived. All you have – all you will ever have – is the breath you are currently breathing.

This breath is your present moment. It is your anchor back into the 'here and now'.

That's why all the meditations in the 28 Day Meditation Challenge begin with gently focussing on your breathing. This slows your thinking down, allows your adrenals and other stress responses to relax and brings you back to the here and now.

> *By taking good care of the present moment, we take good care of the future.*
> Thich Nhat Hanh

Even if you're not feeling stressed, you can still benefit hugely from regular practise of mindful breathing throughout your day. It can help you move into the present moment much more easily. And the more you practise, the easier it gets. It has a subtle, yet profound, impact on all aspects of your experience of life.

If you'd like a way of remembering to practise this technique, while you're sitting at your computer, there's a lovely meditation timer bell from the team at Fungie. You can set it to go off whenever you want to, while you're at your computer (see day 9).

Whether you use an online bell, a reminder on your computer, your phone or another method, each time the bell rings / reminder goes off, you could do 5-10 mindful breaths, using the technique from this week's meditation audio.

If you're not into bells, you could remind yourself to do it each time you sit down at your car's steering wheel – or even while you're on the loo! It can really cut your stress levels, throughout your day. Plus it's easy, it's free and it takes almost no time to do.

Day 17

What more could you ask for?

Namaste,

Clare

P. S. Tomorrow we'll be looking at how wiggling your butt can help you meditate. Yes, you read that right.

Day 17 Affirmation

I choose to breathe mindfully and return to the present moment with a gentle smile.

DAY 18

HOW WIGGLING YOUR BUTT CAN HELP YOU MEDITATE

No, I'm not joking!

Day 18: How Wiggling Your Butt Can Help You Meditate

Earlier in the 28 Day Meditation Challenge, we talked about a senior executive who was too stressed to meditate and was sent away to do deep relaxations every day for a number of months. Only then was he able to learn how to meditate.

By now, we've sussed that being able to relax is essential for being able to meditate. If you're stressed or tired, your meditation won't be as enjoyable or effective as when you're feeling fresh and awake. But often we don't have the time to do a deep relaxation, yet we still want to meditate.

What can you do?

Wiggle Your Butt!

You can shake out the stress. This is a really useful – and somewhat unexpected - technique that I use in face to face classes and workshops with meditation and mindfulness students.

> *Note: please stay within your safe range of movement! You know what is comfortable for you and there's no point in injuring yourself.*
> *If movement is difficult for you, then you can imagine or visualise yourself doing these exercises, for a similar wake-up effect.*

1. **Put some music on that you can't help but bounce to.**
   Choose something that brings a smile to your face and inspires you to dance.

2. **Stand up (ideally!) and start with your fingertips.**
   Wiggle and shake them in time to the music. Then shake your hands and your wrists. Flick your fingertips as though you are flicking the stress away, flicking away the worries, flicking away the tension.

Day 18

3. **Move the shaking up your arms.**

   You can do one arm at a time or both arms. Really give them a shake and a wobble, dancing to the music. Nobody's watching. Nobody cares what you look like!

4. **Then, keeping the arms going, move on to your feet and legs.**

   Try to stand on one foot (you may need to balance against a wall), flicking the stress and tension out of your toes, your feet, your ankles, your legs, your knees - all the way up to the hips. Do the other leg. Smile and let the tension and the stress go, as you shake it out.

5. **Then wiggle your backside!**

   Shake the tension out, wiggle your hips. Jiggle your waist. Wobble your shoulders. Move to the music!

6. **Gently move your neck and face.**

   Be very gentle with your neck, moving it slowly, to loosen and release any tension. Then screw up your face tight, hold it for a moment and then let it go.

7. **And finally… laugh!**

   One of the best ways to release stress and tension, to allow you to relax, is to laugh. So while you're dancing, laugh out loud. If you can think of something funny and really laugh while you are doing all this, then go for it! Don't worry about feeling self-conscious, just laugh as you shake out the stress and tension.

   Even if you start by faking it, you'll soon find the laughter gets your endorphins flowing and helps you to feel happier.

You will be amazed at how even two or three minutes of this will completely shift your mood.

Then meditate.

Day 18

> Being relaxed, but alert, is the key to being able to meditate.

You might be wondering, *"How can I meditate, if I've just been jumping up and down?"* Well, by spending the first few moments of your meditation allowing your body to settle and relax, then practising acceptance, you'll find yourself naturally relaxed and alert - ideal conditions for effective meditation.

This settling process is the same one you have been using at the start of your daily meditation, for the last few weeks.

If you've shaken out the tension and woken yourself up, smiling and laughing to get the endorphins going, you'll find you enjoy your meditation session much more than if you come to it stressed and beat yourself up over the fact it didn't work.

So if you are too tired to meditate, stick on some music and shake it out.

Day 18

Remember, you can be mindful as you do this. Really focus on the movement in each part of the body, giving your mind a break and being fully 'present' to the physical sensations.

Namaste,

Clare

P. S. Tomorrow we're dealing with the 'meditation hump'.

Day 18 Affirmation

I enjoy preparing for my meditation time.

DAY 19

GETTING OVER THE MEDITATION HUMP

How to stay motivated, no matter what.

Day 19

Day 19: Getting Over The Meditation Hump

Around this point of a meditation journey, you're very close to having created firm foundations for your new habit. But it can be easy to feel discouraged - particularly if you're not yet making the progress you had expected. (Remember Day 14 on the power and danger of expectations?)

Often the excitement of the first couple of weeks wears off and this is the phase where you might need to show consistent effort and persistence. It can feel as though we have reached a 'plateau' - a 'hump' - that you somehow need to get past – it's where abhyasa comes in (remember day 12?). But... **The plateau is in your mind.**

Your body will be noticing the difference that regular meditation practice is making. Your emotions will be starting to settle. Even your mind will be learning that it's worth going along with this ride. But we are so used to telling ourselves stories that discourage us when we're making changes, that our mind may continue with its usual job.

We're used to criticising ourselves and judging our progress. In fact, many of us have tried that for most of our lives. But it doesn't work, does it? So how about trying something different?

Instead of following the usual procedure of beating yourself up and continually comparing the progress you're making against some hypothetical standard, how about dumping the drama?

How about turning the spotlight on to acknowledge the changes that have been taking place; the progress you are making? How about looking for the positives on this journey, rather than allowing your old story to leave you feeling disheartened?

Remember: mindfulness is all about moving back into the present moment, and being able to tell the difference between what is 'real' and what is our mind's 'projection'.

How about applying mindfulness to your experience of your meditation journey?

Day 19

> *Yesterday's practice is done. Tomorrow hasn't arrived yet. The only 'real' time you have to experience your meditation is right here, right now.*

So how about trusting the process and simply accepting whatever comes today, rather than trying to force things? This is the magic key to really enjoying your meditation - and making more profound progress.

> *It's funny - the less hard you try, the easier it becomes!*

Are you making it too difficult?

Meditation doesn't have to be difficult. What can seem hard is cultivating the habit of consistent effort - keeping going, even on days when you don't feel like it. True meditation is about being alive to the present moment, in full awareness, and it takes practice. Many of us try too hard to meditate; we take it too seriously. But once you have got the basic techniques under your belt, your practice works best by being as effortless as possible.

> *Relaxed concentration is the key when you're meditating.*

As long as you have relaxed at the beginning, the next stage is acceptance. If your thoughts come up, accept them. Don't engage with them; don't tell the story; don't chat with them; don't send them away - just let them naturally fade.

And when you are focusing and concentrating, the more often you gently and lovingly bring your mind back to the task you've chosen, the more naturally it will tend to rest there. Gentle concentration, relaxed concentration is the key to meditation. That's one of the reasons we relax first. Not only does it make the body more comfortable but it also relaxes your mind. A relaxed mind is much easier to guide than a stressed one.

Day 19

Are you trying too hard? I've written a bonus article on this for you, in case you'd like some extra help:

"Are You Trying Too Hard?"

www.28DayMeditationChallenge.com/bonus

It's funny - the less hard you try, the easier it becomes!

Do you need to work on your concentration?

Concentration is one of the things I used to find hard when I first started learning to meditate. And I have seen it is a common problem for my meditation students, during their early stages of learning how to meditate. It is so easy to give up, because your mind wanders. But gentle concentration and focus makes a huge difference.

Multi-tasking is the enemy of concentration, yet it's a skill that we value highly, in our society... Concentrating on just one thing at a

Day 19

time is looked down upon, yet it helps you get more done - and hence finished - with less stress. There's a key to improving your concentration when you're learning to meditate. And it's simple:

> *You don't have to wait until you're meditating to practise concentration.*

In fact, the more you practise it when you're not meditating, the easier meditation will be and the more progress you will make. You will enjoy your meditations more and they will have a wider-reaching impact on your life.

Honing your concentration skills 'little and often' (even just a couple of minutes, several times a day), will produce noticeable results in a short space of time. And the bonus is that concentration practice is also mindfulness practice. So the act of practising concentration, to help with your meditation, becomes a form of meditation itself.

Here are some simple concentration exercises you could build into your day, without taking up extra time:

- Do the 'taste your tea' exercise from Day 16.
- Actually taste your food when you eat - gently resting your concentration on the flavours.
- The next time you pick up a pen, spend a few moments concentrating on what it feels like in your fingers.
- The next time you cook something, close your eyes for a few moments (at a safe point!) and really notice the smells in the room.
- Close your eyes for 60 seconds and allow yourself to become fully aware of the sounds around you.
- Find a clock or watch with a ticking second hand and rest your attention on it gently, counting the number of seconds before your mind wanders.
- Stop at various points during your day and do 5-10 mindful breaths, really allowing your focus to gently rest on the physical experience of breathing.

Day 19

- Do the raisin mindfulness concentration exercise. This is a great (and classic) mindfulness technique. It involves the simple act of eating a raisin and, once you have done it, chances are you'll never look at raisins the same way again! There's a bonus video to talk you through the process. You'll find the link to the video at www.28DayMeditationChallenge.com/bonus

Awareness, concentration and the ability to focus are skills you can cultivate. It's not difficult; it can change your life.

If your mind wanders, bring it back to the task - without criticism; without judgement; without drama. The more often you can practice relaxed concentration in day-to-day life, the easier meditation is and the more you'll find you really enjoy the results that you see. Practising mindfulness techniques, outside of your meditation time, is a wonderful way to improve your focus and concentration. Imagine the impact that could have on your life!

Namaste,

Clare

P. S. Tomorrow we'll be dealing with handling things that interrupt our meditation – no matter how busy you are.

Day 19 Affirmation

I enjoy finding opportunities to practise concentration throughout my day.

DAY 20

HOW DARE YOU INTERRUPT MY MEDITATION!

The key to good meditation, no matter what's going on around you.

Day 20

Day 20: How Dare You Interrupt My Meditation!

By this stage, I hope you're really enjoying your meditation time - and perhaps even looking forward to it each day. Those ten minutes are special time - 'you' time; your de-stress & 'tune in' time.

So when something interrupts our meditation time, it's easy to get even more irritated than we normally would. Whether it's the kids yelling, our partner bashing and crashing in the background, loud music from next door, cars racing past, it doesn't matter. Those interruptions can feel like a huge deal when you want to meditate.

That's when it's time to remember the three keys to meditation:

1. Relaxation
2. Acceptance
3. Focused concentration

Acceptance is in there for a good reason!

Not many of us have the advantage of being able to go to a retreat centre every day, to sit somewhere in a soundproofed room that's completely comfortable and just the right temperature, with no aches or pains anywhere in the body, and a quiet mind, before we start meditating. It's quite a shopping list of pre-requisites, isn't it?

So, at some point in your meditation practice, you're going to need to learn how to accept what's going on outside - and inside - to be able to experience results from your meditation. And the sooner you work on 'acceptance', the easier you will find meditating.

(Just imagine the impact this could have on the rest of your life!)

> *One of the students on the online version of this course (www.28DayMeditationChallenge.com) found she was getting really cross with her family making so much noise, while she tried to meditate. The kids were playing noisily and her husband had the radio on, while he was washing up.*

Day 20

Working with 'acceptance' (as well as asking for the help she needed – a little bit of quiet – day 5) helped her to move past these irritations and take her meditation to the next level.

In practical terms this is why it's so important to allow yourself that space to settle and relax, at the beginning of a meditation. That's why we take the time to accept the aches and the pains of the body, if there are any; to accept the sounds around you; to accept what the room feels like; to accept those itches and niggles that crop up during your meditation time.

Then, when you've relaxed and accepted your environment, body and mind, you can more easily move into your state of focused concentration. Accepting an outside interruption is no different to accepting an internal thought. It comes and it goes. It only throws your meditation practice if you engage with it and allow it to.

> When a distraction comes up during your meditation, use it as a chance to practise acceptance.

Day 20

> *I remember where I did my formal meditation teacher training, up in an amazing centre in North Wales (www.DruWorldwide.com), and it had an extra-special 'acceptance-tester' for us trainee meditators. The Dru team live in the most beautiful Welsh valley in Northern Snowdonia, but there are regular fighter jet low-level flight practice runs along the valley.*
>
> *Imagine the scenario: you're sitting there, in absolute stillness, and then suddenly the sound of a roaring fighter jet comes racing past at what feels like roof level. The first few times I was there, it used to jerk me out of my meditation. I would start getting grumpy and feeling irritated, thinking, "But I just got relaxed and I just focused and it's not fair!" (Cue a toys-pram-throwing tantrum moment!).*

And my meditation master used to tell a story of a time when he ran a taster course for parents at a school.

> *The parents had been getting very distracted and they'd been shuffling and fidgeting, during their meditations. Whenever there were sounds around them, he really noticed that most of them had lost their concentration and focus.*
>
> *So he taught them how to accept; he allowed them to practise, he explained how to let go of the interruptions; and they made good progress.*
>
> *Then, in one session, there was a fire alarm. He knew there wasn't a practice scheduled for that day, so he opened his eyes and looked round the room. But nobody was moving. He kept looking, still nobody was moving. Everybody was in such a state of acceptance that they were able to ignore the fire alarm.*
>
> *Of course, he had to bring them all up from their meditative state and get them out of the place! But it was a beautiful demonstration of how well they had managed to relax, accept distractions and move into that focused concentration space.*

And I learned from that story.

> *Once I really practised acceptance, the sound of the jet plane came*

and went, without dislodging me from my stillness. People could cough and sneeze in the room, without me getting irritated. My body could send me aches and itchy moments, without me needing to intervene. I no longer needed to tell myself a grumpy story about it. I didn't hang on to it. I didn't really notice it any more. I just got on with meditating.

So, if a distraction comes up when you're meditating, if the phone goes, if the kids are shouting, if a dog barks, if next door is slamming a car door, that's ok; use it as a chance to practise acceptance. How about choosing to feel grateful for it, rather than irritated?

It is how it is. And that's ok.

And just imagine the knock on effect this will have in the rest of your life!

I hope you are enjoying your week 3 meditation.

Namaste,

Clare

P. S. Tomorrow we'll be looking at how to handle the 'old emotional stuff' that regular meditation can bring up.

Day 20 Affirmation

I use each interruption as a chance to practise acceptance.

DAY 21

MEDITATION STIRS THE POT

Emotional first aid and the art of letting go.

Day 21: Meditation Stirs The Pot

Some people cheekily call meditation 'navel gazing'. There's something about sitting around, with eyes closed, allegedly coming up with profound insights, that provokes a sense of the slightly ridiculous in those who haven't yet tried it.

Although meditation techniques can include looking at your life, your reactions, your emotions, your behaviours and your thoughts, it isn't about 'navel gazing'. You're looking at all those aspects of yourself with a clear intention. Through these practices, you are choosing to set ourselves free from the habitual way we normally live life; to see the truth of how things really are; to reclaim your choice about how we experience life; to reconnect with that divine spark, deep within.

When we are in that quiet, still space of relaxed, accepting, focused concentration, we can find that our habits, our beliefs, our assumptions may come up for questioning. It helps us to have more clarity in life and to be able to spot where we're telling ourselves 'stories', rather than basing our decisions on 'truth'. And this new level of self-awareness can cause the 'pot of emotions', deep inside, to have a bit of a stir.

> *It's vital to our happiness and inner peace to really have clarity about what's real and what's just our projection.*

Regular meditation can bring about focused observation of our own habits and behaviours. It awakens a desire within us to be able to choose how to respond, rather than being at the mercy of uncontrollable auto-pilot emotions and stress, as we react to life. This can mean that when you get good at meditation - when you're able to access that still point - the old habits, behaviours and beliefs that no longer fit with who you really are can come up for examination. Depending on how you've been experiencing life so far, some of that might be quite uncomfortable.

Some people might find, for example, that they've had a habit of

Day 21

feeling irritated or angry very easily and that regular meditation practice can bring that to the fore.

> *I remember, when I was starting my 'real' meditation journey (rather than just doing guided visualisations or deep relaxations) that I often found myself feeling more irritable and angry than usual. This had the knock-on effect that I would beat myself up, because - of course - I was meditating every day and I'm an NLP trainer, so 'how dare I' feel irritated? I was supposed to be 'blissed out' and happy, not grumpy and snappy. I was 'supposed to' know better.*

Well, there is no such thing as 'supposed to', for a start! And, secondly, the meditation had allowed me to get myself to a place where I was ready to handle the causes of why I was walking around feeling irritable and angry. At some level, I had made an unconscious decision that I was ready to deal with the triggers for those emotions - and suddenly nearly everybody around me became an Oscar-winning actor, helping to 'press the buttons' for me. Their behaviour helped me see the games I was playing, the stories I had been telling myself and the habits I had created, to keep me stuck with those emotions, over the years. (Thanks guys!)

This is a very common situation on a meditation journey.

The danger, if 'stuff' comes up (and it doesn't matter which emotion it is), is that you can end up projecting your anger / irritation / sadness / annoyance / guilt / regret onto other people. For example, you might snap at the next person who crosses your path when, in reality, your emotion was nothing to do with them. It's like your experience of life becomes overlaid with a movie of that emotion, changing your view of what's really going on.

> *"Meditation is not meant to help us avoid problems or run away from difficulties. It is meant to allow positive healing to take place." Thich Nhat Hanh*

Day 21

> It is vital to our happiness and inner peace to have clarity between what's real and what's just our perception.

Meditation is about learning how to stop being carried away by past pain and regrets – to stop running away from our problems – to stop being lost in despair about the present time or worrying about our future.

Regular meditation practice helps us to realise that we have a choice: to feel angry or to feel happy. It helps to make that choice easier.

> *If you catch yourself experiencing a strong emotion that is clouding the reality of what is happening, practise your mindfulness.*

Here's a really useful technique for times when you need to process uncomfortable emotions:

Day 21

Emotional First Aid Technique

This technique is all about using your breathing as an anchor in a storm of emotions. It helps you to rest; to stop; to reflect; to heal.

1. Bring your focus back into your physical body.
2. Be present, without telling the story, without engaging with the emotion, without resisting it.
3. Breathe. Really focus on your breathing.
4. Breathe out the emotion, breathe in calm and a sense that all will be ok. It works! Keep going, until you feel a sense of relief.
5. If you need someone's help, get it! You don't have to do this on your own.
6. Be kind to yourself, open your heart, and perhaps ask:
   - "What would love do, right now?"
   - "What would kindness say to this emotion, this habit, this belief?"
   - "What would 'courage' or 'trust' say or do?"

   They might sound like strange questions, but if you let the answers bubble up, without critique, then you might be surprised by your insightful answers.
7. Don't judge yourself. Just observe whether it is one of your old auto-pilot programmes that is causing you to react the way you are used to. Perhaps your deepest being is trying to tell you that this is not who you are anymore? You don't need to keep doing that - which means you're getting the chance to set yourself free from that old habit.

This short technique can work in under a minute, once you're used to using it. It will work for you unless, at some level, you're unconsciously choosing to hold on to the emotion; if you don't want

Day 21

to let go of the story...

It helps you to release the emotions, so you can move back to a level of clarity that helps you to see the difference between the story; the drama; the projection; and the truth of the situation. It helps you see 'what's real' about whatever has been going on.

If you'd like some more 'emotional first aid' techniques, there are links to more in the bonus resources for this book. One is a deeper-acting emotional first aid process, similar to the one above. Another is a guided visualisation, which is specially designed for emotions and memories that keep coming back. It is designed to help you gently, but effectively, release the old story and move towards the future.

Links to these techniques are at:

www.28DayMeditationChallenge.com/bonus

Meditation is a wonderful way to reach that still point, so you can see those habits for what they really are: just habits.

Those old habits are not real - you can't pick them up and wrap them in paper and tie a bow on them. You can let them go.

All you need to do is choose.

And if you choose from a position of love and kindness towards yourself, instead of anger and beating yourself up over it, you are much more likely to enjoy the process of letting go of that old habit.

If you find that meditation is stirring the pot for you, make sure you get the support that you need to let go of whatever that habit or emotion is that's been coming up - and then celebrate letting it go.

Wishing you a wonderful meditation today,

Namaste,

Clare

Day 21

P. S. Tomorrow we'll be discovering the secret of kindness, to help you set yourself free from the past and create a beautiful future.

Day 21 Affirmation

I choose to set myself free from old habits that no longer serve me.

Week Four

Welcome to week four!

This week we're moving on to another form of meditation, which combines the elements of the past three weeks with a mantra – a special word or short phrase.

When you are in a mindful, meditative state, mantras can be a powerful way to shift your state of consciousness and to make changes in your life – gently but effectively.

In this week's messages, we'll be talking about the secret of kindness, the most dangerous word a newbie meditator can use, two little words that could change your life, how to tell whether you're 'actually meditating', finding the time, creating a special meditation space and ideas to help you continue with your meditation journey.

Enjoy!

Namaste,

Clare. ♡

DAY 22

DISCOVERING THE SECRET OF KINDNESS

How to set yourself free from the past – and create a beautiful future.

Day 22: Discovering The Secret Of Kindness

Welcome to week four.

This week is the final week of the 28 Day Meditation Challenge. Can you believe you've made it through 21 days already? Well done!

How has it been going? Which bits have you been enjoying? What have you learned?

This week we're going to be moving on to a meditation that is about resting in your heart. It is about accessing the calm kindness, the loving kindness, the gratitude that exists naturally within each of us, but is often drowned out by our voice of worry and stress. It's also about creating a sanctuary space that you can go to, whenever life feels stressful or you're worried, anxious or scared.

But what is kindness?

It's an abstract concept. How do we feel when somebody behaves kindly towards us? And how do we feel when we behave kindly towards them? Often, in our modern western society, we behave kindly, with an 'agenda'. We might be kind to somebody because we want something back from them.

> *"If I am kind to him, he will say yes about such and such."*

And yet true kindness is unconditional. It's about behaving in a way that we know is kind, even if there is no direct benefit for us. Kindness comes from love. It comes without attachment. It comes without agenda. We do it because we choose to.

The Dalai Lama shares a lovely quote:

> *"Whenever possible choose kindness. It is always possible."*

What interests me about this quote is that he doesn't talk about 'being' kind. He talks about 'choosing' kindness. He is telling us that kindness is something we can **choose**. It is always within our

Day 22

power. It is an option that is always open to us. In those few words, he shines a light on all our excuses and habits for not behaving kindly - to others or towards ourselves...

It is perhaps one of the most challenging things we can think of: if somebody behaves really unkindly towards us, responding with kindness. That doesn't mean we are accepting their behaviour. But it does mean that we can choose to allow our thoughts, our feelings and our reactions to come from our heart, rather than from the pain or fear that might have been caused.

> Whenever possible, choose kindness.
>
> It is always possible.
>
> HH DALAI LAMA

We are allowing ourselves to feel compassion towards the actor, even if we strongly disagree with their actions. The two are separate.

*There is a difference between the person
and their behaviour.*

Day 22

Regular meditation helps us to calm our Monkey Mind, making it easier to respond to unkind behaviour from a place of wise equilibrium, rather than emotional pain. It helps us to detach from the drama and the story. It helps us to develop compassion towards the other person, who must be in a place of emotional pain, in order to behave in that way.

When your body and mind are at peace, behaving kindly towards others becomes easier. When body and mind are at war, kindness becomes a great challenge. Meditation helps you move towards your place of inner peace.

> *Being kind to ourselves, as well as towards others, is essential if we're on a journey towards inner peace.*

Accepting who we really are, letting go of trying to change ourselves, letting go of beating ourselves up, ceasing to pretend that we're someone we're not, behaving kindly towards our bodies, behaving kindly towards our minds - all of these choices are open to us, when we are making the changes in our life that meditation brings.

If you've been beating yourself up for decades, it probably hasn't done you much good. How about changing tack and being kind to yourself, instead? And just notice the difference it makes!

When you focus on kindness and the many, many different opportunities we have in a day to practise it and experience it, kindness can become the filter through which we perceive our experience of life. And that can be transformational.

Week 4 Meditation

You can find this week's meditation at Track 4 of the MP3s (or optional CD) which accompany this book. As usual, the transcript is in Appendix A.

Day 22

I really hope you enjoy this week's meditation. It's one of my personal favourites and it's an honour to be able to share it with you.

Namaste,

Clare

P. S. Tomorrow we'll be looking at the most dangerous word you can use when you're learning how to meditate.

Day 22 Affirmation

Today I choose kindness: kind thoughts, kind words, kind deeds.

DAY 23

The Most Dangerous Word A Meditator Can Use

Discover how 3 little letters can scupper your success.

Day 23

Day 23: What's The Most Dangerous Word A Newbie Meditator Can Use?

We have all worked on making changes in our life, over the years. And we all have our own favourite ways of making change work - or perhaps sabotaging it - even without realising. But there's one little word that can throw away all the efforts you are making to change. And it's only 3 letters long.

Want to know what the most dangerous word is, when you are learning to meditate or pick up any other kind of habit? This three lettered word slips into our conversation, without us noticing.

It is. . . cue drum roll…

'Try'

- I'll try to meditate each day.
- I'll try to do ten minutes.
- I'll try to remember to do it.
- I'll try to learn the technique.
- I'll try to let go of being attached to my thoughts.
- I'll try to taste my tea.

What happens when we say the word 'try'?

Just think each of those sentences through for yourself for a moment and notice the physical reaction - there will be one - somewhere in your body. Though it's subtly different for each of us, there's a common theme.

The word 'try' allows us to 'half-pretend', when we're going to make changes. It is as though we're not really committed. Saying "I'll try to do something," allows the option of not doing it. In fact, more than 'allowing', it almost 'encourages' or gives us permission not to achieve our goal. Even saying these phrases in our mind - just

Day 23

thinking them - rather than saying them out loud, has the power to impact our results. We are using our thoughts to programme our mind with our truly intended outcome - just like a SatNav.

Of course, we always have choice, but if we say, "I'll try to meditate this morning," deep down we know there is a strong likelihood that we won't do it. We haven't really made the choice.

We aren't really committed.

What's the answer?

The answer to this is very simple. Instead of, "I'll try to meditate this morning," you can use phrases like:

"I choose..."

I choose to meditate this morning.
I choose to do ten minutes or more.
I choose to notice the difference it is making.

This isn't about an 'either-or' scenario. It's not about forcing yourself to make the change. It's about opening up your choices; opening up your options. Yes, something might still get in the way and you might not do your meditation today, but if all you've said in your unconscious mind is, "I'll try", then your Monkey Mind knows it has got your permission not to bother! And if you've made a commitment and you want to meditate today, then 'try' is not the word you want to be using.

Of course this applies in anything we want to do in life:

I'll try to get the report done by the week-end.
I'll try to remember to call you tonight.
Please try to remember to email me.

> *'Try' is like Monopoly's 'get out of jail free' card, permitting us to pretend we're going to do something, without really having to make that commitment.*

Day 23

> My invitation to you today: stop trying and just do it!

'Trying' is a way of saying, "Yes, but probably no."

The way we think and the subtleties of the language we use in our thoughts have a big impact on what we actually experience and create. 'Try' isn't your friend most of the time. You might like to consider waving it goodbye.

If there's anywhere else in your world that you're using the word 'try' on a regular basis, you might like to look at that situation. Maybe you're resisting something?

Maybe you've not really bought into the commitment? Maybe your unconscious mind is trying to tell you that you don't really want to be doing it?

Day 23

I've written a short bonus article for you if you'd like to know more about making conscious choices. You can find it at:

➡️ www.28DayMeditationChallenge.com/bonus

Play with other phrases you could use instead of 'try' and notice how this simple change can make subtle and yet powerful shifts in your experience of life.

My invitation for you today, on Day 23 of the 28 Day Meditation Challenge, is to stop trying and just do it!

I hope you really enjoy your meditation today.

Namaste,

Clare

P. S. Tomorrow we'll be talking about the magic phrase that can change your life.

Day 23 Affirmation

I allow my choices to help me stay committed on my meditation journey.

DAY 24

TWO LITTLE WORDS THAT CAN CHANGE YOUR LIFE

A simple technique that can transform your world.

Day 24

Day 24: Two Little Words That Can Change Your Life

You may be wondering by now why there's a 'thank you' in the meditation this week. Have you noticed how it feels, doing that part of the meditation? Have you been experiencing resistance to it? Have you been diving in and enjoying it?

It tends to have a bit of a 'Marmite[1] reaction', when you first do it: you either love it, or you don't.

So why are we using 'thank you' in this week's meditation?

The answer is simple.

> *When we whinge and complain, we feel bad. Not only does it affect our emotions, but also our body, mind and spirit.*
> *Complaining makes us tense up and can lead to 'dis-ease', which can lead to disease – physically, mentally and emotionally.*
> *It also programmes our mind, at an unconscious level, to look for more things that are wrong, to support our 'preferred way of thinking' - i.e. complaining.*

It's a truth in life that we tend to get what we think about. Just like me with my driving lessons, in a previous message (I used to drive towards whatever I was looking at), so it is with life. If we are talking about, and therefore focussing on, what is bad or wrong, or might be bad or might go wrong, then that's what we're steering ourselves towards. It's what we're setting our radar to notice.

Moving to thinking from a place of gratitude, rather than dissatisfaction, is a subtle, yet transformational, shift.

It really doesn't matter if you're not feeling like saying "Thank you!" It doesn't matter if you can't think of anything specific to say thank you for. In fact, it works much more effectively if you just repeat the

---

[1] Marmite is a brand of yeast extract spread for toast, in the UK. It is famous for the 'love it or hate it' way people feel about it.

Day 24

'thank you' without anything in mind to say thank you for. Why? Because that would be connecting with your 'thinking mind' and this exercise is about engaging your heart, not your head. It also makes our 'thank you' conditional, because we are effectively saying, "Thank you for this, but perhaps not for that."

So repeating 'thank you' will help you relax into opening your heart.

> *The simple act of genuine, unconditional gratitude has the power to change your life. And what better time to practise it than when you're concentrating – when you're meditating?*

It sets the 'filters' your mind uses to choose how to experience life. You will notice more of the things that are good, beautiful and going well. At a deeper level, it helps us to learn how to feel grateful, even for the things that perhaps aren't quite to our taste, which is an incredibly useful life skill, especially if you are on a path of spiritual development. And **genuine gratitude puts a smile on your face, much more easily than grumbling ever could**. So you'll find yourself wandering round with a spontaneous, gentle smile. And we all know the knock-on effect that can have for us and those around us.

What if you don't like it?

When doing this week's meditation, you may find that there is resistance to saying thank you - and that's ok. If you're experiencing that, just accept it, but keep saying thank you. After a point, that resistance will reduce and the power of your thank you will start to shift your mood, your body and your mind. When you have got into the rhythm of this meditation, you may find that there is a tangible shift in your heart area, as the power of the word allows you to connect with the love and gratitude - and even joy, deep inside you. This is, perhaps unbelievably, our natural state of being.

Day 24

The grumbles and complaints that run through our minds are merely symptoms of the hectic, stressful lifestyle that most of us lead. These grumps mask our true, inner radiance. The thank you process is a way of uncovering it again, so you can create a pathway back to it. And, like any pathway, it needs to be walked regularly, to prevent it from becoming overgrown again.

Walking a path once may dent the grass, but it soon springs back. Walking it several times starts to flatten the grass. But walking it every day, even for a few moments, eventually creates a path that is clear and easy to follow.

And so it is when you tread the path to reconnect with your true nature.

> The simple act of genuine, unconditional gratitude has the power to change your life.

This practice doesn't have to wait for your meditation space. **You can use it as a mindfulness practice**, anywhere, any time. If you're

Day 24

feeling tense and stressed, tread that path. If you're feeling rushed and disconnected, tread that path. If you're feeling sad or lonely, tread that path.

> *It doesn't matter 'who' you are saying thank you to. It doesn't matter 'what' you are saying thank you for. All that matters is that your 'thank you' becomes genuine and heart-felt.*

If you'd like to take this practice deeper and nurture heart-felt gratitude as part of your daily experience of life, you could join us over at The Miracle Of Gratitude: www.MiracleOfGratitude.com

Wishing you joy, love and gratitude in your heart, today and every day.

Namaste,

Clare

P. S. Tomorrow we'll finally be getting back to that question of 'what on earth does meditation feel like?', from the 'Getting Started' section.

Day 24 Affirmation

Today I choose to say 'thank you' – for everything.

DAY 25

HOW DO I KNOW WHEN I'M MEDITATING?

It's about time we answered this question...

Day 25

Day 25: How Do I Know When I'm Meditating?

You might remember from back in the 'Getting Started' section that I shared how I hadn't realised I had never really meditated before, despite 20+ years of practice, until I started to train to be a meditation teacher. I had done plenty of great deep relaxations and guided visualisations, but I had never really meditated.

How did I know?

Because once I knew the techniques to help me 'really' meditate (the kind of stuff we've been covering over the 28 days of this challenge), the experience I had of meditating was very different - much deeper and more still - than the experiences I had had of deep relaxation.

A previous 28 Day Meditation Challenge participant asked the great question, "***How do I know when I'm meditating?***"… and now you have been practising for 3½ weeks, I thought it was time to give you some answers.

Why didn't I answer the question before?

Because expectation is the greatest enemy of meditation!

If I had told you to expect to see, hear or feel something specific, you would either have found your very accommodating unconscious mind creating an experience that 'felt a bit like it, but wasn't really it', or you'd have felt like a failure, if you didn't feel what I said you 'should'.

The thing with meditation is that it feels different for each of us.

Some people find they have visions and insights. Some people find they 'see things' or 'get messages'. Some people experience nothing, other than the stillness. Some find it tough to get past the distractions of the chattering Monkey Mind.

Day 25

None of this is wrong or right. It just is. Comparing your experience with that of others, and then judging yourself (or them!), isn't helpful. It becomes an issue when we get attached to a particular way of experiencing meditation. "But I didn't get to see such-and-such this time!" or "But I didn't get that glowy feeling in my heart this time!"

Disappointment is the likely outcome and that's not the reason why you're choosing to meditate, I'm guessing.

> *The problem with expectation is that it confines our meditation experience to be inside a box, limited by that expectation.*

If we expect to have visions, then we set our unconscious mind's filters to watch for them, and we're likely to miss other aspects of our meditation, because they're not 'on our radar'.

Expectation is the greatest enemy of your meditation experiences.

Day 25

The other challenge is that **each meditation we do is different**. If we get attached to a particular experience, then we're making it harder for ourselves to accept whatever comes the next time, if it's not the same. **Remember, the second step of meditation is acceptance.** That means practising acceptance of your experience of meditation, as well as everything else! When you have decided that acceptance will be your focus, then you open yourself up to experience the full beauty of your meditation - whatever form it happens to present itself in that day.

If you ask people who are used to meditating regularly, they will have many different ways of experiencing meditation. But there's likely to be a common theme.

Meditation includes a sense of stillness.

> *There's an ancient metaphor that describes the mind as being like an ocean. The waves can be wild and stormy at the surface, but deep down there is always a gentle, flowing calm, which cannot be disturbed by even the most violent storm.*
> *We tend to give our focus to the incessant chatter and turbulent emotions at the surface, forgetting that the deep stillness is there for us to reconnect with, whenever we choose to.*

Whether it's the mind, the body, the emotions or even something deeper than that, meditation brings a sense of stillness and peace with it.

With gentle practice, this stillness - this peace - can last beyond the end of your meditation time. It can start to help you ride the waves of the rollercoaster of life and feel centred and grounded (and happier!), no matter what is going on.

Whatever meditation has been for you, so far, is just perfect. And, if you keep meditating, your experience of it next year will be different to this year. It changes over time, as you hone your skills and learn to let go and trust.

Day 25

> **Quick Exercise:**
>
> I'm curious:
>
> How would you describe 'meditation', so far?
>
> What have you experienced over the past 3 ½ weeks?
>
> How has your experience of meditation changed?
>
> Want to share? Want to find out how different it is for others?
>
> Please pop by our Facebook page:
>
> www.Facebook.com/28DayMeditationChallengeCourse

I really hope you're enjoying your week 4 meditation.

Namaste,

Clare

P. S. Tomorrow we'll be looking at more techniques to help you sort things, if you're still finding it hard to fit in your meditation time.

Day 25 Affirmation

I enjoy discovering anew, each day, what meditation and mindfulness feel like for me.

DAY 26

STILL STRUGGLING TO FIND TIME TO MEDITATE?

A final truth that can help you magically create more time.

Day 26: Are You Still Struggling To Find Time To Meditate?

We often end up feeling guilty about taking time out for ourselves, even for something as beneficial as meditating. This can happen whether you've got a busy life, with family, work, friends and others that you normally give your time to, or if your time is your own.

Taking time to do things for yourself, having 'you' time, is something we've allowed ourselves to be conditioned to believe is bad. And yet, if we don't take this time out to recharge; to reconnect with that inner still point; with that inner peace and happiness, the huge risk is that we'll experience burnout. And then we'll be absolutely useless to those around us. In fact, we'll become a burden.

> *If you think about batteries, we wouldn't expect the batteries in our camera or phone, to keep working forever and ever and ever, without recharging them. We pay attention when the warning light tells us they're running low.*
> *Yet when we put the batteries on to charge, we don't resent them; we don't tell them off; there's no "How dare you run out of energy, batteries!"; we don't try to talk them into feeling guilty! And we all know it's much easier to top up the charge levels before they get too low - and before we need them for a big event.*

Yet we do very little to charge our own batteries, as we go along. We wait until they go flat, until we have flu, until we have sinusitis, until we have something that really knocks us off our feet and into bed.

Regular meditation, mindfulness and deep relaxation practice can transform your energy levels.

Meditation can reduce your stress levels. It can help you feel happier and calmer. You will find that you are recharging your

Day 26

batteries as you go along through life.

This happiness and this sense of calm become contagious to those around you, so that those who need your help will enjoy the experience of being around you even more. And you will enjoy sharing your time with them, because you know you are topping your batteries, every day.

So why on earth do we allow ourselves to feel guilty about taking those ten minutes?

> Regular meditation, mindfulness and deep relaxation practice can transform your energy levels.

If you are genuinely finding it hard to accept finding ten minutes a day for yourself, it's an issue that is important to look at. If you find you're not really interested in meditating, that's absolutely fine! I suggest you give yourself a break and stop trying. Or, if you do want to meditate and you're still not finding the time, there may be deeper issues running. Perhaps you need to pump up your 'why'?

Day 26

(Remember the 'How to stay motivated' exercise on page 36?)

You - and your health - are worth ten minutes a day. You're worth so much more than that. And you don't have to jump through any particular hoops to meditate; it's simply about choosing.

I choose today to take the time to meditate... because...

... Remember your 'because' from the beginning of the course?

Remember why you're doing this and accept that it's absolutely OK to take time out for yourself. Then just do it! Don't bother about waiting for the 'right time' or the 'perfect conditions'. Just do it! You know you'll feel so much better afterwards.

I really hope you enjoy today's meditation.

Namaste,

Clare

P. S. Tomorrow we're looking at how to keep yourself motivated, beyond the 28 days.

Day 26 Affirmation

My health and happiness are worth ten minutes of my time. I choose to meditate today.

DAY 27

HOW TO KEEP YOURSELF MOTIVATED.

Secrets for keeping the momentum going, after you have finished these 28 days.

Day 27: How To Keep Yourself Motivated

You're nearly at the end of your four week meditation challenge!

Has it gone quickly? How are you finding it? Today I'm talking about how to keep yourself motivated, right now and then beyond the 28 days.

The Secret Key

When we're learning a new skill or a habit it's easy to keep ourselves motivated, once we've started to experience results. So your job is to make sure you're noticing them.

Here are some ideas you could try out today.

Make sure you're actually open to seeing the results you're getting. Often they're there in front of us, but we don't spot them, because we're expecting something else. So maybe it's worth taking a few moments today to think about how taking part in the 28 Day Meditation Challenge has helped to change your life, so far.

> **Quick Exercise:**
> - What impact have the last 4 weeks had for you?
> - How have your emotions been going?
> - How have you been feeling physically?
> - How has your behaviour changed?
> - Are you noticing it's easier to carve out your daily ten minutes to meditate?
> - What do you notice, if you miss your meditation?
>
> How about sharing your answers?
>
> www.Facebook.com/28DayMeditationChallengeCourse

Day 27

Allow yourself to notice the progress you're making! We're often too busy to spot it.

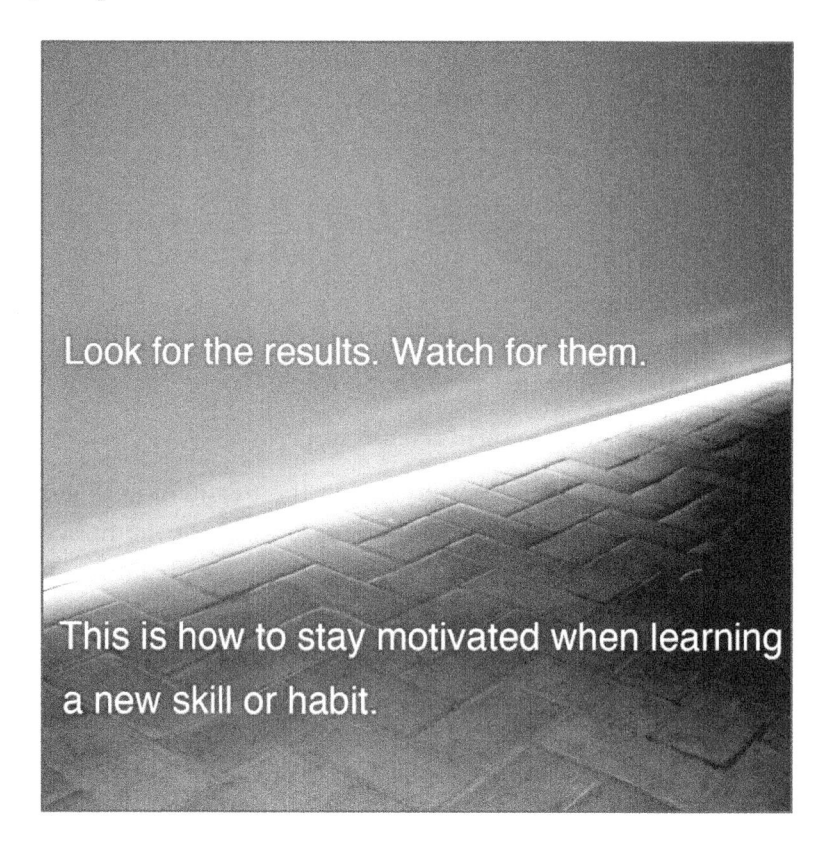

> Look for the results. Watch for them.
>
> This is how to stay motivated when learning a new skill or habit.

Other key strategies at this stage:

- **Don't aim too high.**
  Keep it realistic and don't make too big a deal of it if you miss a day (or three!). Learn from it and move on, as we covered earlier in the 28 days.

- **Start small and build on it.**
  To be honest, ten minutes a day really isn't so much to ask of yourself. If someone told you to meditate for an hour, twice a day, that would be unrealistic for most of us, without making dramatic lifestyle changes. But to find ten minutes, which is enough to start making a difference, is absolutely possible.

Day 27

- **Buddy up**
  Maybe you'd like to have a meditation buddy, a friend that you're following the 28 Day Meditation Challenge with?

  They can hold you accountable. You could text or phone or message each other when you've done your daily meditation and share the progress that you're making.

- **Remember you *can* concentrate.**
  If you're finding it hard to concentrate, don't give up. Concentration is a skill that we need to relearn. Yet concentrating is something that comes naturally to us: just look at a young child when they get absorbed in a task. You can call their name, over and over, but they can't hear you, because they are lost in their task.

Quick Exercise:

Think about the times in the past where you were changing something and you hit what we call 'the wall', and yet you kept going. When you got to the other side, you realised you had made a leap in your skill level.

How did you feel afterwards?

How did you keep yourself motivated?

What worked for you?

What didn't?

If you could imagine a future you that has made it through the next few months and years, what advice would you give to the 'you' back in the 'here and now'?

You did it then, you can do it now! The key is to keep going; to keep choosing.

Day 27

Staying motivated is about allowing yourself to see the results you're getting and to keep gently, consistently going with the routine of your daily ten minutes (or more!) of meditation.

And on Day 29 – after the 28 days are done – I'll be sharing some final ideas on how you could keep your new meditation habit going.

I hope you really enjoy today's meditation.

Namaste,

Clare

P. S. Tomorrow we'll be talking about creating a sanctuary for your meditation space – and how this can help you keep going with the habit.

Day 27 Affirmation

I enjoy noticing the progress I am making – each meditation counts.

DAY 28

Creating A Sanctuary For Your Meditation.

Supporting your meditation habit, no matter how busy life gets.

Day 28

Day 28: Creating A Sanctuary For Your Meditation

Wow! It's the final day of the 28 Day Meditation Challenge - can you believe it's day 28? It's absolutely wonderful that you've made it through the 28 days. I'm hoping that you have enjoyed the journey and that you would maybe like to keep meditating in the future…?

It is my deepest wish that these 28 days have awakened an excitement within you, to be able to connect with that sense of peace and calm; that still point; that point of being; that point of truth; that point of clarity deep within yourself. And I also hope that you've been enjoying the space you've created for the 'you' time.

If you want to stop after today, that's completely ok. Remember, there's no judgement here. And each meditation counts.

If you want to keep going, tomorrow there will be a final message that explains different ways you can keep your meditation journey running. Yes, I know it'll be day 29, but I didn't want "What's next?" to get in the way of "What's now?" It will cover ideas ranging from finding local classes (and 10 questions you should ask the teacher, before joining!), through to online courses and even how you can create your own meditations.

But, for today, I would like to talk to you about **creating a sanctuary for your meditation space.**

Before we dive into the details, I've got a few questions for you, about how you have been meditating over the past 28 days.

> Quick Exercise:
>
> Have you been meditating in the same place each day?
>
> Or have you tried different places?
>
> How did they compare?
>
> Are there some places where it's easier?
>
> Did you notice anything, if you returned to the same place, each day?

Day 28

When we meditate in the same place every day, that place builds up a really special energy; you can feel it, as soon as you sit down. And it makes it much easier to meditate. Our mind enjoys consistency and familiarity and soon gets anchored into habits and routines. Having a single place to meditate is a very quick way of getting back into the physical, psychological and emotional 'meditation space'.

If at some point during the day we're feeling stressed, tense, worried or upset, if we just go and sit for a few moments in that space, it can bring us back to that inner still point. It can help us to let go of the emotions that we don't really want to be holding on to, even when we're not meditating.

The dictionary describes a 'sanctuary' as being:

> *'a room or other place where one can seek refuge from his everyday concerns; a haven.'*

Sounds like a great place to meditate?

How to create your sanctuary.

There is no right or wrong way to create that sanctuary - and there's no one saying you have to! But millennia of meditators have found that setting up a special place to meditate makes it easier and more enjoyable. Your own belief systems, your upbringing, your values, your religion, your spirituality will dictate the kind of things that you might like to place in your sanctuary area. It can be amazingly powerful to create even just a tiny corner of your home that is your meditation space.

> *Always keep it clean; always keep it clear of clutter; don't use it for anything else.*

It might be the top of a book case, a shelf or even a box in a corner with your seat in front of it (the seat can move, if you need it to,

Day 28

during the day). Perhaps you might like to put things on it that have a special significance for you, which reminds you of that inner calm or perhaps of the beauty of nature. You could choose something that inspires you. It might be a beautiful photo. It might be a flower. It might be a crystal. It might be a leaf. It might be a book. It could be a collection of things.

It is not about worshipping those objects in any way. This is about creating a space that is just for your meditation, which you don't use for anything else, because it builds up a special energy. By returning to your special meditation space with the intention of reaching your still point, day after day:

> *You'll find your still point is there waiting for you before you have even sat down.*

As soon as you decide to walk towards it, your brain will automatically trigger the neurological pathways that help you to remember what it feels like, setting off the chemical reactions for relaxation in your body.

> *It gives you a 'zero effort' head start to your meditation.*

And there's another bonus to setting up a sanctuary space, while you're creating a meditation habit: **it nags you!**

If you've been putting off your meditation that day, it will call to you, each time you walk past it or catch sight of it, out of the corner of your eye. So it becomes a gentle reminder to give yourself that ten minutes!

If you can't create a space - if you're living or working somewhere that you don't have that option or are travelling a lot - then maybe you would like to get yourself a special shawl or a blanket or a cushion - something that you associate with your meditation? Choose something that is special, which doesn't get used for anything else. Then it will remind you that you're heading to your meditation sanctuary, each time you pick it up.

Day 28

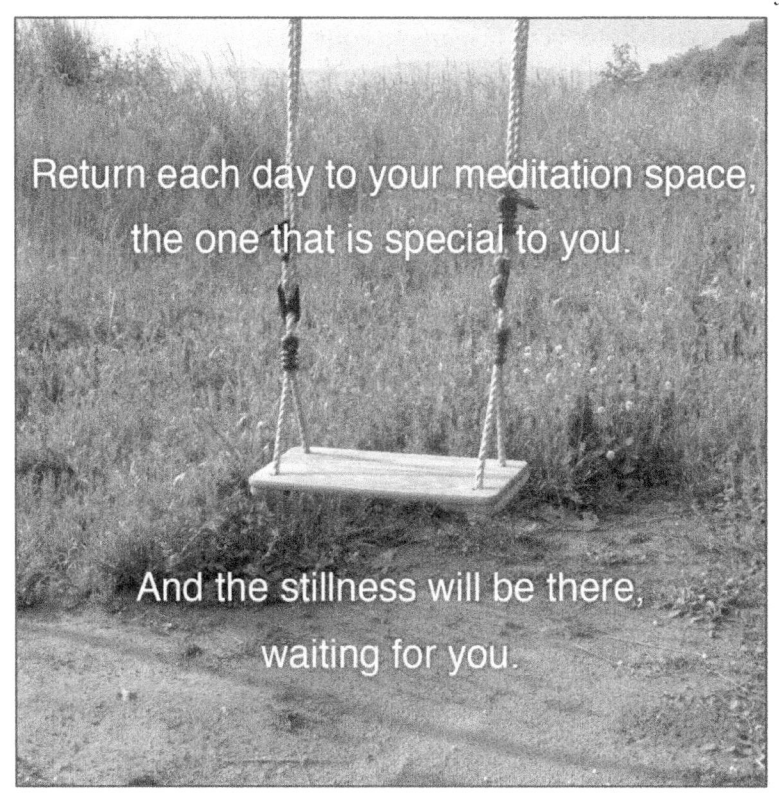

> Return each day to your meditation space, the one that is special to you.
>
> And the stillness will be there, waiting for you.

Use your nose!

If space is at a premium, then your meditation sanctuary could be a smell, instead of a place. It's no coincidence that so many traditions use incense and other fragrances, as part of their spiritual ceremonies.

Our memories are stored using our senses, so seeing an image, hearing a voice, tasting a flavour, feeling a texture or smelling a scent can instantly – and automatically – transport you back to a previous memory, complete with that memory's emotional, mental and physical state.

The sense of smell is the most primal way of doing this, due to its link to the most ancient part of our brain – the hypothalamus. Smells bypass the 'thinking mind' and trigger memories fast. So using a particular incense or aromatherapy blend each time you

Day 28

meditate will help you fast-track your way towards feeling more calm, relaxed and alert – ready for your meditation practice.

This is known as 'anchoring'.

For a reminder on how anchoring works, remember the bonus article:

> **"How To Use Anchoring To Help With Your Meditation"**
>
> www.28DayMeditationChallenge.com/bonus

As soon as you decide to walk towards your meditation space – or light your incense or smell your chosen aromatherapy blend, it triggers your anchored meditation 'zone'. Your brain will automatically trigger off the neurological pathways that help you remember what it feels like, setting off the chemical reactions for alert relaxation in your body. It gives you a 'zero effort' head start to your meditation.

Creating a sanctuary for your meditation, creating a special space or having a special shawl or cushion, really helps you to honour that part of you deep down inside that wants you to 'come home'.

Creating your sanctuary – your special meditation space – is such an important part of cultivating a long-term, sustainable meditation practice that the Vietnamese Zen Master Thich Nhat Hanh has recently written a whole book on the topic. It's quick to read, beautifully illustrated and, of course, inspiring.

You can find links to it in the bonus section on the website.

I really hope you enjoy Day 28 today.

It has been an honour to share this journey with you.

As I said, I'll be back with a message tomorrow, with suggestions for how you could keep your journey going.

Namaste,

Clare

P. S. Remember – there's a final message tomorrow, on Day 29, to help you figure out what you want to do next. See you there!

Day 28 Affirmation

I choose to create a special place for my meditation.

And Finally...

DAY 29

What's Next?

Ideas to help you continue with your meditation journey.

Day 29: What's Next?

Obviously, it's up to you whether or not you want to continue with your meditation journey. But, just in case you do, here are some suggestions that might help.

1. **Let's connect on Facebook**
   Join us on the 28 Day Meditation Challenge Facebook page and connect with others who have enjoyed this book.
   www.Facebook.com/28DayMeditationChallengeCourse

2. **Want to do it again?**
   You could choose to repeat the 28 days. Students who have done this find that the messages, exercises and meditations work at an even deeper level.

   Perhaps you could do it with some friends this time? Or maybe join in with the online version of the course. You can find out more at: www.28DayMeditationChallenge.com

3. **Want to take things to the next level?**
   How about joining in with our **'Soul-Sized Living'** community? As a member, you can choose to receive:
   - **a new guided meditation audio each month**
     to help keep your meditation practice fresh and inspirational
   - **regular email messages**
     to help keep you on track and to remind you to meditate!
   - **exclusive articles and meditation resources**
     to help you deepen your experience of your meditation & mindfulness practices, as well as making changes in your life
   - **membership of our private online community**
     where you can join in with the discussions, get moral support, share your meditation experiences and get answers to your questions

   To apply to join, go to: **www.SoulSizedLiving.com**

Day 29

4. **Find a local class**

    If you live near Forest Row in East Sussex, UK, you could join in with one of my regular face-to-face meditation classes. There are also weekend seminars and workshops, if you live further away.

    You can find details at:

    www.ClareJosa.com/workshops

    If you're not local to Forest Row, but want to find a good meditation teacher, I have written an article that will help you:

    "Looking For A Meditation Class? 10 Must-Ask Questions For Newbie Meditators":

    www.28DayMeditationChallenge.com/bonus

    And, to give you an idea of the kinds of answers you should be looking for, I've written a second article with the answers I would give. This is at the same link. I hope these help!

5. **Want to do an online course?**

    I have created a range of online courses that you might enjoy – from a 10 week mindfulness course (*How To De-Stress With Mindfulness*), through to *6 Weeks To Spring Clean Your Life* and even Mastermind Groups, where you can work with me on live calls and Skype workshops. You can find details of all of these here: www.ClareJosa.com/online-courses

6. **Check out some of my other books?**

    I have written a number of other books that might be of interest to you, if you enjoyed this course. I have also created a range of meditation, mindfulness and deep relaxation CDs. You can find an up-to-date list here:

    www.ClareJosa.com/Clare-Josa-Books-CDs

Day 29

Before I sign off, I'd like to say a huge thank you to you for sharing your journey with me.

No matter how often you meditated or how far you got, each time you meditated or practised mindfulness will have taken you a step closer towards the life you want. None of it is wasted. It all makes a difference.

It is amazing – and humbling - how many people have already joined in with the 28 Day Meditation Challenge- and how many are joining in with it.

Thank you so much for being part of it.

Wishing you inner peace and happiness on your journey.

With love, Namaste,

Clare. ♡

www.ClareJosa.com

www.Facebook.com/28DayMeditationChallengeCourse

Appendix A: The Meditations

The four meditations are used for a week each.

The idea is to go through them slowly, so that they last about 10-12 minutes.

They will work most easily for you if you record them and play them back. Where you see ……. the idea is to leave a pause of up to 30 seconds.

The meditations will also work for you, as a guide, if you just remember the process and do it in your head.

The meditations are included on the MP3s (or optional CD) that accompany this book. If you would like to download MP3 versions here's where you will find them:

www.28DayMeditationChallenge.com/bonus

Appendix A: The Meditations

Meditation 1

Sitting comfortably in a chair or on the floor, make sure your back is fairly straight, your neck is gently lengthened and your chin is slightly tucked in. Allow your eyes to softly close, with a gentle smile on your face.

Spend a few moments just scanning through your body, giving each part permission to start to relax... relaxing your feet... your calves... your shins... your knees.

Relaxing your thighs... your buttocks... your abdomen... your back... all the way up to the shoulders.

Your arms... your hands... your fingers. Relaxing your neck... your jaw... your face and even your scalp.

Now, allowing your breathing to slow slightly, I'd like you to take three breaths, in through the nose and out with an "Ahhh" ... relaxing as you release the breath. Breathing in – and out – "Ahhh". One more time, breathing in – and out – "Ahhh".

Allow your body to start to settle, giving it space for any fidgeting or shuffling to die down, as you find yourself sitting comfortably... and today's meditation focuses on our breath.

To begin with, I'd like you to imagine that you can breathe in from deep in the earth beneath you and as you breathe in from deep in the earth, you breathe that groundedness all the way through your feet, through your bottom where you're sitting, up through your spine, all the way to your chest area.

And as you breathe out, allow that energy, that groundedness, that breath to float upwards and out through the top of your head.

And then imagine with the next in breath, you're breathing in through the top of your head to your chest and breathing out all the way down your spine into the earth.

And just continue that gentle breathing cycle. In from the earth, up through to the chest. Out up through the top of your head. In through the top of your head to your chest and back out and down

Appendix A: The Meditations

into the earth. And continue that in your own time for the next few moments

… . . . …
… … … … … … … … … … … … … … … … … … … …

And, when you're ready, allow your breathing to settle in your abdomen. In your belly. And this isn't the time to be holding your stomach muscles in. We are going to do a few moments of belly breathing. As you breathe in, allowing your abdominal area to expand. As you breathe out, allowing it to gently contract.

… . . . …
… … … … … … … … … … … … … … … … … … … …

And with each in breath, breathing in relaxation, and with each out breath, breathing out any stress or tension or worries.

… . . . …
… … … … … … … … … … … … … … … … … … … …

And allow your breathing to be gentle. There's no need to force it. There's no need to control it. Allow yourself to become the silent observer of your breathing. The next few moments, allow your focus and your awareness to gently settle on watching your breath. Breathing in relaxation and breathing out tension.

… . . . …
… … … … … … … … … … … … … … … … … … … …

And if your mind wanders, that's ok. Gently guide it back to watching your breathing.

… . . . …
… … … … … … … … … … … … … … … … … … … …

Allow your focus to rest gently on watching your breathing. Don't force it. Gently guide your mind back to becoming fully aware of your breath in your abdomen.

… . . . …
… … … … … … … … … … … … … … … … … … … …

Appendix A: The Meditations

And if your body is trying to distract you with any aches or grumbles, that's ok too. Allow yourself to make shifts if you need to and then bring your focus back to rest gently on observing your breath.

… . . . …
… … … … … … … … … … … … … … … … … … … …

When you are ready, allowing your breath to deepen as you prepare to draw yourself back from this meditation … breathing in energy and breathing out any tiredness. Becoming fully aware of your physical body as you are sitting. Starting to wiggle your toes, wiggle your fingers. Starting to stretch. Maybe having a bit of a yawn – releasing any tiredness and knowing that any time you might be feeling tense or stressed or worried today, you can come back just to focusing on your breathing.

And to finish off, giving your face a good rub, rubbing your hands together, shaking your arms, eventually standing up and stamping your feet a bit to make sure you are completely back in the present moment fully grounded and ready to continue with your day. -- END —

Appendix A: The Meditations

Meditation 2

Welcome to your Week 2 meditation.

Sitting comfortably on a chair or on the floor, we'll begin with three deep-sighing breaths where you breathe in deeply – and breathe out with an "Ahhh – "AHHH", releasing your tension. Breathing in – and release "AHHH". Breathing in – and let go "AHHH".

And spending a moment letting your awareness move around your body, become aware of where the tension is and gently allow it to release, allowing your body to settle, making any minor adjustments you need to make so you can sit comfortably. Allow your eyes to softly close, with a gentle smile on your face.

And then allowing a gentle wave of relaxation to move up through your feet, your ankles. Warm, gentle relaxation through your calves, your shins, your knees, your thighs, your buttocks, your lower back and abdomen. Gentle relaxation flowing up your spine, your torso, your chest, your shoulders. Flowing through your arms, out through your fingertips. Gently allowing your neck to relax, your jaw to relax, your cheeks, your ears, your eyes.

Allow that gentle wave of relaxation to flow over your eyebrows, your forehead and your scalp. And as your body settles relaxed on the chair or floor, imagine there's a string gently pulling through the top of your head straightening and lengthening your spine, gently lengthening your neck and tucking your chin slightly under, making sure your shoulders are relaxed.

For the next few moments, I'd like you to do the breath we did last week.

Breathing in from the ground deep beneath you, all the way up through your body to your heart. Breathing out through the top of your head. Breathing in through the top of your head back to your heart, your chest area and breathing out into the earth beneath you. And continue this at your own pace for the next few moments.

… . . . …
… … … … … … … … … … … … … … … … … … … …

Appendix A: The Meditations

Allowing your breathing just to settle now into a natural, gentle, relaxed rhythm, allowing the body to be relaxed and still and turning your attention this time to your thoughts. It's time to become a silent observer of your thoughts. For the next few moments, I invite you to become aware of your thoughts. Not to engage with them. Not to enter into a discussion with them. But just to notice what you notice when you willingly and gently let your awareness rest on your thoughts.

… … … … … … … … … … … … … … … … … … … . . …
… … … … … … … … … … … … … … … … … …

And notice whether your awareness, whether your attention, was able to stay resting on your thoughts, or whether, in contrast to last week, your awareness was taken to your body instead of your thoughts. And if you find yourself getting distracted, gently guide your focus back to being the observer. A non-engaging, non-resisting observer of your thoughts.

… … … … … … … … … … … … … … … … … … … . . …
… … … … … … … … … … … … … … … … … …

And sometimes it can be hard not to engage with our thoughts. If you're finding that's the case, you might like to imagine that your thoughts are on a conveyer belt, and just as they arrive, they travel gently across your awareness, disappearing at the other side as you watch them go. So for the next few moments, perhaps play with the idea of your thoughts being on a conveyor belt – they flow through, whether you interact with them or not.

… … … … … … … … … … … … … … … … … … … . . …
… … … … … … … … … … … … … … … … … …

And for the next few moments, how about experimenting with the idea of your thoughts simply being clouds floating gently past in the sky. And by not interacting with them, by accepting them and observing, just like clouds on a breezy day, they'll gently float into your awareness and away again.

… … … … … … … … … … … … … … … … … … … . . …

Appendix A: The Meditations

… … … … … … … … … … … … … … … … … … …

And when you're ready, you might like to really focus on your thoughts and for the next few moments, without engaging in any story, without any discussion, allow yourself to slow your thoughts down. If they're racing, if they're distracting, simply tell them – "Slower" – and notice what you notice.

… . . . …
… … … … … … … … … … … … … … … … … … …

And when you're ready, you might like to play with telling your thoughts to become quieter. If you notice they're interrupting you, they're louder than you'd like, simply tell them in your own way – "It's time to be calmer and quieter" – and then step back and observe, accepting whatever you notice.

… . . . …
… … … … … … … … … … … … … … … … … … …

Thanking your thoughts for joining in this meditation with you, it's time to bring yourself back to the physical body, to start gently wiggling fingers and toes, giving them a stretch, moving your back, perhaps a nice big yawn – "Ahhh" – and then rubbing your hands together to get the palms of your hands nice and warm and then cupping them over your eyes – your gently closed eyes. Warming your eyes, refreshing your eyes and leaving your hands in place, opening your eyes behind your hands, gently spreading your fingers apart, letting the light back in gently until you move your hands away from your face. Give your face a good rub. When you're ready, stand up, stamp your feet, shake yourself awake and welcome back. Well done.

--END—

Appendix A: The Meditations

Meditation 3

Welcome to your Week 3 meditation.

To begin, we'll start with three sighing breaths – breathing in to the belly, breathing out with an "Ahhh", "AHHH". Breathing in again – and releasing "AHHH". One more time, breathing in – and let go of any tension "AHHH".

And allow yourself to settle in a position that allows you to be comfortable and relaxed yet alert. With your spine quite straight and imagining that cord pulling you up through the crown of your head, gently lengthening the spine, lengthening the neck, tuck your chin slightly under, making sure the shoulders are relaxed, and for the next few moments, allow your awareness to travel round your body, allowing each part of it just to gently relax. Allow your eyes to softly close, with a gentle smile on your face.

Relaxing your feet, your ankles, calves and shins. Relax your knees, your thighs, your buttocks, your lower torso. Relaxing your upper chest and your back and your shoulders. Relaxing your arms, your hands and your fingers. Relaxing your neck, your throat. Relaxing your jaw. Relaxing your cheeks, your ears, your eyes, your eyebrows. Releasing any tension from your forehead. Relaxing your scalp. And allowing yourself a few moments of stillness just to let the body settle.

… . . . …
… … … … … … … … … … … … … … … … … … … …

And as you've done before, breathing in through the earth, up through the base of your spine or your feet if they're on the floor, breathing all the way up to the heart, breathing out through the top of your head, breathing in through the top of your head to the chest area and breathing out all the way into the earth. And continue this cycle at your own pace for the next few moments.

… . . . …
… … … … … … … … … … … … … … … … … … … …

And when you're ready, allow your breathing just to settle into a

Appendix A: The Meditations

natural, comfortable rhythm for you. And with your eyes gently closed and a soft smile on your face, move your awareness, your focus, your concentration to your breathing. Become aware of the coolness of the air as it enters your body and the warmth of the air as it leaves. And for the next few moments just rest, paying attention to the physical sensations as you breathe in and breathe out.

… . . . …
… …

And if your mind wanders and thoughts creep in, smile at your thought and acknowledge it, and move your focus back to the physical sensation as you breathe.

… . . . …
… …

And as you keep your mind gently resting, observing your breathing, you might become aware of the gentle movement of your chest and your belly with each in and out breath.

… . . . …
… …

Gently guiding your attention back to your breathing, for the next few moments you are going to gently count your breaths. Counting in one as you breathe in, out one as you breathe out. Mentally saying "In two" as you breathe in again and "Out two" as you breathe out. If you find your mind wanders, acknowledge the thought, bring your focus back to the practice and start again. In one and out one. Without judgement, without attachment.

… . . . …
… …

And if your mind wanders, gently guide it back to the practice, starting again at one. If you can make it to ten, great. Fifteen. If you only make it to one, that's fine too. It's not a competition.

… . . . …

Appendix A: The Meditations

... ...

Releasing the breathing practice, keeping that soft smile on your face, in a moment I am going to ring a bell and I invite you to listen to it with the whole of your awareness and keep listening right to the end of the reverberation and into the stillness that follows.

[RING A BELL HERE – OR IMAGINE ONE!]

... ...
... ...

Allow your focus to be completely absorbed in the sounds. Sounds outside you and perhaps even the sounds inside you.

... ...
... ...

Preparing to release your practice. Bringing your focus back to your physical body. Starting to wiggle your fingers and wiggle your toes, and have a stretch and a good yawn as you fill your lungs with oxygen. Rubbing the palms of your hands together to create a nice warmth. Cupping your warm palms gently over your closed eyes. Opening your eyes behind your closed hands and spreading your fingers slightly to allow the light in ever so gently. Moving your hands away from your face. Giving your face a good rub and when you're ready, standing up, giving your feet a good stamp on the ground, your body a shake and making sure you're completely back in the present moment in the here and now.

--END—

Appendix A: The Meditations

Meditation 4

Welcome to your Week 4 meditation.

We'll begin by getting comfortable, sitting on a chair or on the floor. With your spine quite straight, imagining that invisible cord pulling up through the top of your head, gently elongating your spine and your neck. Tucking your chin slightly under. Allowing the shoulders to relax. And three sighing breaths. Breathing in – and out with an "Ahhh", "AHHH". Breathing in – "AHHH". Breathing in – "AHHH".

Spending a few moments allowing the body to settle. Allow your eyes to softly close, with a gentle smile on your face. Gently scanning around the body for any areas of tension that need releasing. And as you find them, breathing in warmth and relaxation to that area. Breathing out any tension. And just gently scan round your body for the next few moments, allowing each part of it to relax and settle ready for your meditation.

… … … … … … … … … … … … … … … … … … … …
… … … … … … … … … … … … … … … … …

And, when you're ready, bringing your focus to your breathing. Taking your in-breath from the earth deep beneath you all the way up through your body to your chest. Breathing out through the crown of your head. Breathing in through the crown of your head and out down through your body back into the earth, and continue with this cycle in your own time for the next few moments.

… … … … … … … … … … … … … … … … … … … …
… … … … … … … … … … … … … … … … …

And, when you're ready, allowing your breathing to settle into a gentle, comfortable rhythm. For the next few moments, allowing your focus to gently rest on awareness of your breathing in your physical body, without changing your breathing. Without controlling it. Just allowing your awareness to settle on your breathing.

… … … … … … … … … … … … … … … … … … … …

Appendix A: The Meditations

... ...

And if your mind wanders, or your body niggles, accept that's what happened. Gently guide your focus back to your breathing.

... ...
... ...

When you're ready, allow your attention to move to the chest area. To the heart. And for the next few moments, let your focus settle there, noticing what you notice in your chest area as you meditate.

... ...
... ...

Allow your body to be soft with a gentle smile on your lips. Keeping your focus in the heart area, allow a feeling of softness, of warmth, perhaps a golden light to fill the area, ever so gently expanding throughout your body.

... ...
... ...

Don't force it. Just allow that warmth, that softness, the golden light if you can see or feel that, to gently flow.

... ...
... ...

And gently guiding your focus back to your heart. ... . . . For the next few moments, I invite you to silently and slowly say the word "Thank you". Say it in your head, feeling it in your heart. It doesn't matter who you're saying "Thank you" to, or what you're saying it for. My invitation to you is to focus on the word "Thank you". "Thank you", "Thank you". And continue in your own time to say the word "Thank you".

... ...
... ...

And if your mind wanders, smile at it and then gently guide your focus and your awareness back to silently saying the word "Thank

Appendix A: The Meditations

you".

… … … … … … … … … … … … … … … … … … … . . . …
… … … … … … … … … … … … … … … … … … …

And, over time, as you practice this meditation, you'll begin to notice the subtle shifts this practice creates for you physically, in your emotions and in your thoughts. So resting in the gentle stillness for the final few moments, continue to silently say "Thank you".

… … … … … … … … … … … … … … … … … … … . . . …
… … … … … … … … … … … … … … … … … … …

And bringing your awareness back to the physical body, allowing your fingers and your toes to start to move. Starting to move your back and stretch. Stretching your arms, giving them a shake. Perhaps having a yawn – nice deep breath of fresh air – "AHHH". Rubbing the palms of your hands together, creating a nice warmth and cupping them over your closed eyes. Opening the eyes behind your hands, gently spreading your fingers apart. Moving your hands away from your eyes. And giving your face and your scalp and your neck and your shoulders a good rub before you stand up, stamp your feet a bit and make sure you're really back in the present moment. Well done.

--END—

Appendix B: Bonus Articles

I have included a number of bonus articles, to help when you might want to go a bit more deeply into some of the topics we have covered.

By including them in the bonus section or appendix, it means you don't feel too bogged down by overly-long daily messages, but the extra resources are there for you, if you need them.

Some of them are here in this appendix. Others are available on my website.

www.28DayMeditationChallenge.com/bonus

Why Do We Find It So Hard To Get Started?

So it's the first few days of the 28 Day Meditation Challenge and there's a chance you've not started yet. Don't worry – you're not alone!

One of the things we often see at the online forum is people asking for help to get started. It can be tricky to overcome the inertia and get started with making change, in any area of life. It's as though the first day of meditation has become a really big thing for us. As human beings, we're pretty good at building up the proverbial molehill to the size of a mountain.

What's going on? And what can you do about it?

Firstly, there's a good reason why the 28 Day Meditation Challenge only asks you to commit to 10 minutes a day. That's because it's achievable! Just imagine: if the phone were to ring right now, chances are you would answer it and somehow find 10 minutes to handle that call. If you can do it for an unplanned phone call, you can do it for a pre-planned meditation session.

Secondly, it's worth a look at the reason you're putting it off. A common scenario is that people haven't chosen a time. They rush through their day, with the usual panics, dramas and stresses, thinking, "I'll start it in a while, when I've done such and such. " Then we get to the end of the day and it hasn't happened.

> *What's really happening here is that the person hasn't made the commitment. They haven't made the choice to do their meditation.*

Perhaps they're a little afraid of starting the new habit? Perhaps they have unwittingly built the challenge up to be too big a deal in their mind? Perhaps they're convinced that they have more important things to do? (Fortunately the messages, over the 28 days, help you deal with all of this – and more!).

What's the solution? If you realise that you are putting your meditation off, how about stopping, just for a moment, to really think about this challenge and what it means to you. If you can manage to meditate for 10 minutes each day (which you can!), just imagine what it could do for your day-to-day experience of life? Remember your 'why?' from the beginning of the course? Imagine actually achieving that!

Here's what one of the students in the online forum said to herself, in just this situation:

> *"I thought, "Right, I've got to start somewhere and I AM going to start now!". Then I just sat myself down and clicked the link in my message and got on with it. "*

Choosing to meditate for ten minutes really isn't as hard as it seems, especially if you're choosing to use the MP3s (or optional CD) that come with this course. It really does make you feel more relaxed and calmer at the end of it. Within just a few days, you'll find yourself looking forward to your meditation space.

Over at the forum for the online course, I see testimony to the fact that people benefit, even from day one: *"If this is how I feel after my very first attempt, I can't wait to see how I am at the end of the challenge!"*

If procrastination is your thing, then remember the famous sports brand's slogan – and just go and do it! If you're rushing, with too much to do, but you want to meditate – you know your 'why?' – then prioritise it. Make it an appointment in your schedule. Don't allow yourself to compromise. It's ten minutes, not an hour. You can do this! Take that first step. Do it now. Usually, whatever else we feel is more important will wait.

> *It's not a big deal. You can't 'get it wrong'. Just focus on today – not the whole 28 days.*

Remember: the choices you make in this present moment will shape your future. How about doing something, right now, that your future self will thank you for?

Five Things You Need To Know About Meditating On A Chair

Our typical image of someone meditating is of a person sitting on the floor, with their legs twisted into a pretzel shape, with a faux-serene look on their face, disguising the inner agony.

Fortunately, it doesn't have to be that way!

> *Good posture is the key to both comfortable meditation and also staying awake during your meditation.*

When I run my face-to-face classes for beginners, we bust the meditation posture myth by starting off on chairs. There are several reasons for this:

- Not everyone is comfortable sitting on the floor. If you are used to chairs, it can feel stiff and creaky, getting down on the floor. And some people struggle with getting back up.

- Having everyone on chairs makes meditating more accessible. It reduces judgement (of yourself and others), because pretty much everyone can sit on a chair.

- The goal of a long-term meditation and mindfulness habit is to be able to meditate effectively, any time, any place. If you only ever meditate on the floor, like a pixie, you'll get anchored into that posture. This means that you can find it harder to meditate elsewhere.

Being flexible about how and where you meditate – accepting the external environment and factors beyond your control – is one of the keys to inner peace. If your ability to meditate is dependent on a certain sitting posture and location, it will slow down your progress.

That's why I encourage people to learn how to meditate on a chair. Once you've got the process of meditation sussed, it's easier to experiment with different locations and postures.

One thing I never recommend is sitting down on the floor, stressed out from your day, closing your eyes and expecting enlightenment to follow! Good meditation is also about good preparation – which we cover in detail as part of the 28 Day Meditation Challenge.

For the meantime, here are 5 things you need to know about meditating on a chair:

1. **You don't need a special meditation chair.**

    In fact, I don't recommend them. They're rarely made to be adjustable enough for your personal physique. And there's no such thing as an 'average' person. If you come across one that feels brilliantly comfortable and enables you to have good meditation posture, great! But don't spend your time and money searching for one.

2. **Don't bother with an armchair.**

    Although it's tempting to get really comfy when you meditate, a typical armchair is a bad friend to meditation posture. Remember what we said in the day 2 message, about your parasympathetic (relaxation) and sympathetic (fight or flight) nervous systems needing to be in balance, to be able to effectively meditate? Well, a comfy armchair encourages you to relax and slouch so much that your sympathetic nervous system switches onto standby mode and you'll find yourself doing nodding-dog impressions, before you know it!

3. **A dining chair is great.**

    Choose a chair with a firm base, which will help you sit upright and stay awake. You can add cushions to support your back. You can put the phone book under your feet so they don't dangle (like mine!) or a cushion under your bottom so your knees aren't pointing at the sky.

4. **Your back doesn't need to lean against the back of the chair.**

The easiest way to balance your sympathetic and parasympathetic nervous systems is to sit up, without your back leaning on anything. For most of us, supporting our back with the back of a chair will cause us to lean backwards.

Sometimes, if our back muscles aren't very strong or our day-to-day posture is in need of some loving attention, it helps to put a cushion between your back and the back of the chair. But very few people meditate well whilst leaning backwards.

5. **It might feel funny!**

    If you're used to meditating on the floor, it can feel strange meditating on a chair. But that's ok. Just go with it for a week or so. Tweak your posture until you feel upright and comfortable. It's worth the effort, because you can then get back into your meditation position (and be anchored into that sense of alert relaxation) any time you sit on a chair – even at work. Plus it does wonders for your posture.

    If you're used to slouching at the dinner table, then sitting upright on the chair can feel funny. Again, that's ok. So there you have it – 5 things you need to know about meditating on a chair.

If you're part of one of my online meditation classes or courses, please follow the prompts in the recordings at the start of each of your meditations. These are designed to help you to get comfortably into a relaxed, but alert, posture, each time.

Remember: good posture makes a huge difference to your meditation experience. It's worth the practice. Any time you put into it now will pay dividends in the weeks, months and years ahead.

If you have questions about meditation posture or experiences you'd like to share, we'd love to hear from you via the Facebook Page: Facebook.com/28DayMeditationChallengeCourse

How To Contact The Author

If you would like to contact Clare Josa, the easiest way is via her website:

www.ClareJosa.com/Contact-Clare

She would love to connect with readers of the 28 Day Meditation Challenge. You can find her at:

- Facebook www.Facebook.com/28DayMeditationChallengeCourse
- Twitter: @clare_josa
- YouTube: www.youtube.com/user/clarejosa
- Get Clare's free monthly newsletter: www.clarejosa.com/join-soulsizedliving/

About Clare Josa

Clare Josa is a certified NLP Trainer, a formally qualified Meditation Teacher, a Seminar Leader and Executive Mentor who feels passionately about helping people to fall in love with who they really are.

She is the author of numerous books and the creator of a wide range of online courses, as well as face-to-face workshops. They help you to dump your old excuses, let go of limiting beliefs that have been keeping you stuck and to take inspired, practical action towards living the life of your dreams.

Her career began with a Master's Degree in Mechanical Engineering and German, spending a decade in diesel engine manufacturing. But she realised that helping people remember how to feel happier

Connect With Clare Josa

and how to be who they really are was what she most loved doing.

She studied Neurolinguistic Programming (the 'user manual for your brain' / 'Practical Psychology' - NLP), qualifying as an NLP Trainer (training students up to Master Practitioner level) in 2003. She built on her 20-year enthusiasm for meditation by training to become a Meditation Teacher in 2008, as well as continuing her life-long passion for writing and teaching.

Her engineering background means that the inspirational work she shares is always grounded in practical common sense – to which she adds an intuitive and light-hearted approach.

Clare lives in Sussex, UK, with her husband, three young sons and a very bouncy Jack Russell.

Her other books include:

The Little Book Of Daily Sunshine	ISBN 978-1908854407
How To De-Stress With Mindfulness	ISBN 978-1908854575
6 Weeks To Spring-Clean Your Life	ISBN 978-1908854230
The Miracle Of Gratitude	ISBN 978-1908854452
Vibrant For Life	ISBN 978-1908854360
Mindful Moments	ISBN 978-1908854445

Today's choices create your tomorrows.
With each and every thought, you can choose again.
With each and every breath, you can choose thoughts that inspire you and make your heart sing.
Wishing you love and laughter.
Namaste. Clare xx

Made in the USA
Monee, IL
23 December 2020